ENC
v
G
IN
REVELATION

DENNIS LENNON

SERIES EDITORS
ALISON BARR, JOSEPHINE CAMPBELL, TONY HOBBS

SCRIPTURE UNION

Scripture Union, 207–209 Queensway, Bletchley MK2 2EB,
England.

© Dennis Lennon 1996

First published 1996

ISBN 1 85999 035 5

Unless otherwise attributed, scripture is taken from the Holy Bible,
New International Version. Copyright © 1973, 1978, 1984 by
International Bible Society. Anglicisation copyright © 1979, 1984,
1989. Used by permission of Hodder and Stoughton Limited.

British Library Cataloguing-in-Publication Data
A catalogue record for this book is available from the British
Library.

Cover design and illustration by Grax Design Consultants.

Printed and bound in Great Britain by Cox & Wyman Ltd, Reading.

CONTENTS

FOREWORD

Throughout its long history, promoting systematic, daily Bible reading has always been central to Scripture Union's worldwide ministry. At first there were Bible-reading cards that detailed a series of daily readings throughout the year. But before too long comments were published to accompany the notes and, in the early 1920s, a quarterly booklet was produced. It was called *The Scripture Union* with the sub-title 'Daily Notes', the name by which the booklet was to become known.

By the 1990s Scripture Union's promotion of systematic daily Bible reading relied on three separate Bible-reading notes for the English-speaking world. Like *Daily Notes*, *Daily Bread* was widely used over several decades, and these two were joined more recently by *Alive To God* which was launched to offer a complementary approach to Bible reading. All three publications have always had the following in common:

- A commitment to the authority and inspiration of biblical text;
- A conviction that reading the Bible should not merely be a cerebral process; the reader should also be encouraged to respond to what they have read.

Bible-reading notes inevitably reflect the culture and concerns of their time. So, for example, some of the early notes made frequent attempts to summarise biblical passages using three points. Although this was a useful *aide-mémoire*, it did tend to be somewhat forced at times! More interestingly, the notes of the '30s, '40s and '50s – when the evangelical world was struggling with the impact of the implications of liberal scholarship – concentrated on re-stating the basic doctrinal truths. Today the notes reflect a strong emphasis on the importance of applying biblical principles, and the growing interest throughout the Christian world on what can be described as 'spirituality'. This is seen in the increasingly varied forms of worship, the rediscovery of ancient Christian writing and music, and an awareness that responding to God can involve feelings and emotions as well as the mind.

There is much in Christian culture that is exciting and refreshing, but it is taking place against a background of a widespread decrease in Bible reading. It seems that the emphasis on Christian experience – important as that is – is blinding many people to the other side of the Christian life: duty and discipline. Twenty years ago most members of evangelical churches were committed to the importance of personal Bible reading on a regular basis. Nowadays, although many churches would claim to be Bible based, individual members have all too often given up regular personal Bible reading. Bible-reading aids cannot in themselves change this trend. What we must continue to pray for is God's Holy Spirit to provoke whole Christian communities to rediscover the importance and excitement of regular Bible reading – without losing the joy of the variety and depth of Christian experience.

Marrying regular Bible reading with dynamic Christian experience is the aim of Scripture Union Bible-reading notes. Partly to reflect that principle, it was recently decided to change the title of *Daily Notes* to *Encounter With God*. The former described the process but the latter describes the purpose.

Over the years readers have often encouraged us to reprint popular series of the notes. However, we have always been reluctant to do so, partly because writers prepare notes prayerfully and under the guidance of the Holy Spirit for use at a particular time and in a particular way. Numerous stories from readers testify to how a particular note on a particular day met a specific need, and are witnesses to the Holy Spirit's role in the process. Nevertheless, when in the early 1990s we began to deal with entire biblical books in a single series, a formula began to suggest itself: not a reprinting of the series as such, but the series reworked and expanded by the writer; still using the distinctive *Encounter With God* approach, but with the space to develop and explore some of the issues which could not be covered in a 300-word note.

There are a number of things that make Scripture Union Bible-reading notes distinctive, but one element perhaps stands out above all others: beginning and ending with scripture. Starting with the Bible passage, the writer offers thought-provoking comments to encourage the reader to go back to the passage with fresh enthusiasm and new insights, eager to respond with new commitment to what God is saying through scripture: in other words, *to encounter God*. It is the prayer of all who have worked on this series that such will be your experience as you read this book.

Tony Hobbs, Publishing Co-ordinator

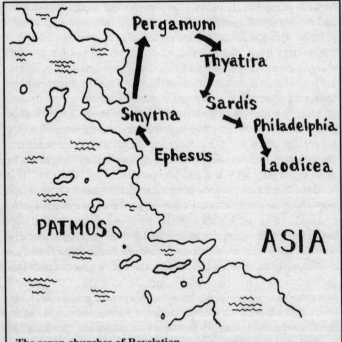

The seven churches of Revelation
A messenger from John in exile in Patmos would have crossed to Ephesus first, and then taken a circular route. In Revelation the seven churches are listed in the order he would have visited them.

INTRODUCTION

Much of the current millennial frenzy is enough to give the Apocalypse, the Book of Revelation, a bad name. Doomsday expectancy is drumming up a lot of business for gurus and false prophets of all stripes. A magazine reports that one cult-church has already moved to the Montana mountains to prepare for 'well, for *something* bad and big. Exactly what is rather vague'.

The very word 'Apocalypse' conjures up ideas of near-total devastation, an end-of-the-world-as-we-know-it scenario. These misunderstandings and the misuse, not to say abuse, of Revelation occur when people take bits and pieces out of it and cobble together theories about the End. Of all the books in the Bible this is the one which simply must be taken as a whole; nothing short of the whole story will keep the reader on track. It is not a collection of weird conundrums, nor is it a cunning end-of-the-world crossword puzzle for fanatics with overheated imaginations. The Book of Revelation is first and last a pastor's passionate letter of encouragement to his churches who were facing imminent severe persecution. We take that as our main interpretive principle. Pastoral letters are intended to be intelligible to everyone and not only to the one or two who happen to have a PhD in semiotics!

John wrote as a pastor and as an imaginative artist, which is a fascinating combination. His images and symbols, codes and numbers, are like abstract figures which the viewer can walk around, seeing fresh meaning from different angles. We must think with the imagination when reading Revelation. The effect is for the symbols to snag in our minds – obscure, teasing, elusive, slipping in and out of focus but, I have discovered, eventually yielding up their extraordinary, awesome power and their sense of otherness. They come to us out of the mysteries of the invisible world where the kingdom of God impacts on this world.

Most of John's symbolism is taken from the Old Testament. Austin Farrer called this method a 'rebirth of images' as John gives fresh power and application to the OT symbols, and does so with startling freedom, breaking most of the usual 'rules' of interpretation along the way. The challenge in reading Revelation is to allow it to tell us how to read it. The danger is that we dictate to the text and say, for example, that of course the thousand years of the millennium means what it says, a thousand years, literally. And yet presumably we would not dream of taking the 'red dragon with seven heads and ten horns and seven crowns on its heads' as a literal snap-shot of the devil. Remember, everything in Revelation is symbolic of invisible spiritual realities. Numbers and cryptograms are part of John's repertoire of symbols. The ones which occur most frequently are as follows.

7

Seven is the number of completeness and perfection. The sevenfold visions of the seals, the trumpets and bowls, indicate a complete series of divine actions operating throughout the present age. One rule of interpretation is that the many unnumbered visions are usually details within a complete seven-fold vision.

144,000

This number and its permutations suggest the pleasing beauty and order of completeness, the perfectly complete and balanced Israel of God. The cubic shape of the city of God (12 x 12 x 12), suggests unity, perfection, reconciliation, harmony.

$1/_3$

This fraction is commonly used to indicate the limited effect of God's discipline in natural disasters, etc, which are intended not to destroy but to lead to repentance.

$3^1/_2$ years = 42 months = 1,260 days

These numbers are taken originally from Daniel's prophecy and indicate 'a time of persecution' of any length. In Daniel it is stated as 'a time, times and half a time' (Dan 12:6–7).

666

Amazing creative imagination has been expended by the experts on this one! The most satisfying of the many interpretations is that if the Greek name for the Emperor Nero, 'Neron Kaisar', is transliterated into Hebrew characters which are then given their numerical equivalents, they add up to '666', the number of the beast.

Finally, I can only say that I have found meditating on Revelation a (literally) amazing experience, quite unlike any other. The progress of the vision to its awesome consummation in the transfiguration of the old creation into the new, floods the current gloom with 'an inexpressible and glorious joy' (1 Peter 1:8).

Dennis Lennon

DOXOLOGY FIRST

Revelation 1

Revelation is world theatre. It is the unveiling of Jesus Christ as Lord of history and of current events. It goes behind history and tells the story from the perspective of the kingdom of God.

Doxology opens this cosmic drama and tunes everything that follows, until all heaven and earth are healed and restored in praise to the Father, Son and Holy Spirit. It is the irrepressible Easter song, bursting through the darkness of deathly human systems like Christ bursting from the grave. It is, said George Herbert, 'A kind of tune which all things hear and fear.' The doxology of the cross and resurrection penetrates every inch, even the nightmare visions of a world gone haywire.

Jesus Christ entered the struggle between God and Satan and won the decisive victory. That is why in the Book of Revelation he is called the Conqueror or Overcomer. God's purposes for his world unfold out of that victory (3:21). What is needed now is that Jesus Christ should win his victory in each one of his people so that they overcome by sharing in his great overcoming. Thus in the Book of Revelation Christians are called upon to be 'overcomers' by their faithful witness to Christ in the face of satanic rage. That is the profound theme of the vision messages which are the Revelation.

Christ for the present moment

Persecution and the real possibility of martyrdom were boiling up over the heads of John's churches on the mainland. A simple action like a pinch of incense in the flame at Caesar's shrine could save a Christian. Would their vision of Jesus be exalted and compelling enough to keep them faithful to him regardless of the consequences? When John sat down to write a pastoral letter to his people (1:4–8), God gave him the very best gift for their encouragement: an apocalypse, an unveiling, a revelation of Jesus Christ, the Overcomer, as never seen before (vs 1–3).

John is not serving up palliative imagery here, in which fragile Christians can escape from the hard facts of the so-called 'real world'. Revelation is profoundly the real world because it penetrates beyond surface phenomena (as seen in the media's presentations) to the struggle at the centre of things. What we are shown there provokes the overflow of thanksgiving: 'to him be glory and power for ever and ever! Amen' (v 6).

The overflow of praise

The Revelation doxology is loaded with Christological content. It is weighty, like the glory of God. Look at three strands of thanksgiving:

'Look, he is coming' (v 7)
Revelation is like a cosmic detective thriller which tells the reader on the first page the outcome of the story. All history is being drawn towards its Omega point when God will judge the world by Christ Jesus, the Saviour of the World. Jesus was killed by the nations for the nations; the coming judge is the man once judged by sinners. History is caught in the gravitational pull of that past-and-future event (22:20).

Christ is the Lord 'who is, and who was, and who is to come' (v 8)
This designation is a New Testament elaboration of God's mysterious name (Exod 3:14). Scholars suggest its root meaning is something like 'The One who brings into being all that is' (including Rome), and the elusive 'I am who I am, I will be who I will be' and not who *you* want me to be! He is the God who is literally 'not yet'. Not yet finished with the world, or with the church or, thankfully, with us personally. He moves ahead, around, above us, eluding our grasp, defeating our pagan need to pin him down and manipulate him for our own ends. He is dancing circles around the Caesars, the despots, the manifestations of dark powers and all

those arrogant concentrations of human energy that would run the world (Rev 1:17–18). God is the source, guide and goal of all there is.

Trust God
Settle your mind once and for all that nothing in the future can take Christ by surprise, nothing lies beyond his mastering reach (1:8, 18). Christ is the Alpha and the Omega. The future is already a familiar story to him since he is the Author of the Play from Act One (Alpha) to the final curtain (Omega). There will always be those tinpot authors who attempt to rewrite the Play (their own little play within the Play). Do not be impressed. They will pass into oblivion soon enough.

> Remember if you can then
> Only the All-Father
> Can change the cast or give them
> Easier lines to say...
>   (W H Auden)[1]

These three strands of the doxology belong together as one. We wouldn't divide them any more than we would divide the sounds in a piece of music, or analyse a kiss. They are ours for singing, praying, laughing, overcoming.

The vision

'On Patmos ... in the Spirit' (vs 9–10). There is a comic side to redemption. John had been detained 'at Caesar's pleasure' on the island of Patmos, an insignificant rock off the coast of Asia Minor and a place for felons. Caesar isolates John only to trigger a stream of visionary messages that lampoon emperor worship and exalt Christ the King!

Why are our own encounters with the Lord not more frequent or more fruitful? Augustine names one reason in his *Confessions:* 'You, Lord, were within me but I was in the world outside myself. You were with me but I was not with you.' God calls, but we are not at home: distracted, restless, greedy for sensations, self-absorbed, unfocused. The old saints thought this a lunatic way of

managing our inner lives, like selling gold for the price of pota-
toes. They said, 'The unexamined life is not worth living. Wake
up, before death wakes you up!'

John turned and saw the Lord 'among the lampstands'
(vs 12–13), a crucial observation which locates Jesus here among
his people, attending to the well-being of his earthly congregations (Heb 4:14–16; 6:16–20; 7:23–26).

Brilliant suns and roaring waterfalls evoke the glory and
energy of the risen Lord (Rev 1:14–16). 'Don't unweave the
rainbow'(G B Caird). Allow the vision to exert its majestic and
emotive power. Better still, go outside, in a storm or to a glorious sunrise; feel and taste it!

'And his eyes were like blazing fire' (v 14; 2:18). In the
Gospels, people felt that gaze. Jesus saw through to their secret
thoughts. He sized up Simon with a glance: 'You are ... You will
be' (John 1:42). We each of us bring what we are and what we
have into our encounters with Christ. It matters that we do, for
that is what we are; and yet in this meeting it counts for nothing,
because we are required to leave what we were before. To meet
Christ is to receive his invitation to give up our personal darkness,
to stand before him as we really are, transparent to his gaze 'like
a blazing fire'. Whether we love and welcome his searching
glance, or hate and avoid it, determines, said Jesus, whether we
are at this moment being saved or being lost (John 3:19–21). Yet
the realisation that we are transparent to his eyes can bring enormous relief. At last we are known. The darkest parts of us, even,
can come out into his light seeking deliverance. No need, now, to
hide. Pretence is pointless. At last we can abandon the disguise
and the phoney accent. There is no one here to impress. Finally,
only one audience matters – the audience of One.

Even more telling than John's awestruck description of the
risen Lord is what it did to him as he felt in his body the over-
powering realities of the present and the future in that dazzling
glance: 'I fell at his feet as though dead' (Rev 1:17).

Looking at John flat on his back we wonder how it is possible
to do business with such a God. Get too close, see too clearly, and
all our circuits go up in smoke. Perhaps it is as well that our powers of spiritual perception are as dim as they are! The unbearable

splendour is screened and filtered out by our sheer secularism. Thus we get by on second-hand reports and the occasional glimmer of glory, and tiny theophanies. Only we should not mistake our myopia for normal sight.

Much more important than our spiritual fickleness and fugitive emotions is the description of the dazzling Lord who left John shattered – he is 'like a son of man' (v 13). We have a friend, a brother for all time, within that consuming fire. 'Son of man' means that Christ crossed over onto our side at his incarnation as one of us, and took on our nature to heal it from within. Hence the reference to the familiar words of the Gospels, 'Do not be afraid' (v 17), and the same healing, restoring touch of those hands which raised up so many despairing people in the days of his flesh. 'Such a high priest meets our need' (Heb 7:26).

A WORD TO ANGELS

Revelation 2 and 3

Flame is a biblical symbol for the people of God. A dependant and derived flame drawing on God's fire, aglow in his radiance, set ablaze by his fiery beauty.

> Thee, God, I come from, to thee go,
> All day long I like fountain flow
> From thy hand out, swayed about
> Mote-like in thy mighty glow.
> > (Gerard Manley Hopkins)[1]

Old Israel knew herself to be 'a light for the Gentiles' (Isaiah 42:6). Her emblem was the golden menorah, the seven-branched candelabrum which illuminated the tabernacle and then the temple (Exod 25:31–40). The Romans walked off with it as a souvenir of their demolition work in Jerusalem in AD70. The New Israel, the church of Jesus Christ, does not possess a menorah; *she* is it. Seven free-standing lamps, each with a star over it (Rev 1:16, 20). The lamps and stars connect and communicate in the living Lord.

If the churches are lamps on earth, the stars are lamps in heaven, the heavenly counterpart of the earthly lamps. Jewish thinking was familiar with the idea of earthly entities having their angelic representatives in heaven, responsible for them before God. John is here adapting this idea. The stars are living and purposeful, they are 'angels' (1:20, lit. 'messengers') whose task it is to keep the lamps in good order with their flames burning brightly in witness towards the world and worship towards God. One further clue: notice that what the Lord says to the angels is, at the end of each message, also described as 'what the Spirit says to the churches' (2:7, 11, 17, etc). Thus the angels are not separate from or independent of their respective churches. They are in and of their churches. So, who or what are these 'angels'?

The angel of a church is its essential self, its soul, heart, will, those powers and faculties operating behind choice and behaviour. They are the 'messengers' through whom God communicates with us and by which we are able to respond to him. In a word *the angel of a congregation is its listening, thinking, choosing, adoring heart.* 'Above all else, guard your heart, for it is the wellspring of life … My son, give me your heart' (Prov 4:23; 23:26).

The seven star-angels (the hearts and minds of the seven churches) are in Christ's right hand as he moves amongst the lamps (Rev 1:16) in a close, protecting, cherishing relationship. He speaks to each one and each time reveals startling insight into the local conditions of that congregation. 'It is not in a mirror that a man recognises himself truly; it is in the call that comes to him and the promise he receives' (Hans Wolff).[2]

John's description of the Lord is next repeated, aspect by aspect, in the seven messages to the seven churches (seven symbolising the whole, universal church). This suggests that in order to see the 'entire' Lord Jesus, and to hear his complete word, we will need to look and listen to the entire church, not just our part of it. Incredible as it may sound, given the mediocrity of so much in the church, we are nevertheless chosen to be the taste and sample, the clue and demonstration, of the kingdom of God. Therefore, normal experience for the church in the world will be 'suffering … kingdom … patient endurance' (1:9). Satan desires nothing better than to discredit the wisdom of God by a poor showing in the church. To each congregation in this war zone the Lord says, 'I know…' Their seven snapshots, taken together, enact the story of the church at any time.

Message to the Ephesians – whatever became of love?

The identity of a church is formed in the tension between what it believes and where it lives, its theology and its culture.

Ephesus was an important city port, strategic enough for Paul to invest three years of his ministry in building the church there (Acts 19; 20:17–37). The traffic of trade, people and ideas flowed through it between east and west. The fabulous temple to Artemis, the mother goddess, was in Ephesus (Acts 19:23–27), and in 29BC the city became closely associated with the Roman imperial cult and the veneration of the emperor as divine.

The Ephesian Christians were wide awake and knew what they stood for. They detected and rejected bogus leaders (Rev 2:2) and the troublesome Nicolaitan sect (more about those in the letter to Pergamum). Their vigorous orthodoxy was their 'deeds, hard work and perseverance ... you have not grown weary' (vs 2–3).

It is fashionable to regard orthodoxy in Christian belief as somehow dull, rigid, safe and defensive, while offbeat teaching and heresy is perceived as creative, courageous, warm, imaginative and even exciting. Yet Dorothy Sayers could say, 'There was never anything so perilous or so exciting as orthodoxy, nothing so sane and so thrilling.' Heresy reflects the way people would like things to be rather than the way God has provided. False teaching is a form of oppression because instead of building up life and faith in vital communion with God, in the end it leads people into confusion, despair and death (a recent book is titled *The Cruelty of Heresy*).[3] False doctrine appears to be a matter of the intellect only, but it proceeds to enmesh the whole moral and spiritual life.

To their great credit the Ephesians unmasked the sources of error and dealt with them. Yet they come in for severe censure: 'You have forsaken your first love' (vs 4–5). Not their love for Christ, surely, since they wholeheartedly defended his truth against distortion and refused to compromise with an attractive and powerful paganism. But somewhere along the way the warm, beating heart of love had chilled and died. Without the generosity and big-heartedness of love, their admirable critical qualities became harsh, sharp, judgemental, a suspicious spirit. They are sound but cool, orthodox but aloof. Repentance is imperative at Ephesus, a return to their original, overflowing generosity when they first tasted Christ's intoxicating love.

How can we return to love? Only by loving. Not by introspective analysis, since love lives away from itself and does not know about itself. It is self-forgetful as it lives towards other people ('Lord, when did we see you hungry and feed you?', Matt 25:34–40). Thus love can, says Barth, 'playfully overcome the dark temptation which tries to overcome love in people who love' (Rev 2:7). The dark temptation is, of course, to become self-absorbed about our love!

We cannot expound the meaning of love. We can only point to it and recognise it for what it is. Newman's charming picture of love describes a sort of servant-minded, gentle courtesy, an unselfconscious concern for people which could work a quiet revolution in many of our congregations:[4]

> He never inflicts pain ... he is mainly occupied in merely removing the obstacles which hinder free and unembarrassed action of those about him ... he is like an easy chair or a good fire which do their part in dispelling cold and fatigue ... he carefully avoids whatever may cause a jar or a jolt in the minds of those with whom he is cast ... makes everyone at their ease and at home ... he is tender towards the bashful, gentle towards the distant and merciful towards the absurd ... he observes the maxim that we should ever conduct ourselves towards our enemy as if he were one day to be our friend.

At Ephesus the 'overcomer' (v 7) is a person who overcomes that supreme contradiction in terms, a loveless orthodoxy.

Message to Smyrna – eternity now

Smyrna was a resurrected city rebuilt on the coast after the destruction of the original city in 600BC. As one of Rome's oldest allies, Smyrna claimed the title of First City in Asia. Christ knows what it is costing his people to be faithful – 'I know your afflictions and your poverty' (v 9) – and signs himself, 'the First and the Last, who died and came to life again' (vs 8; 1:17–18).

Jews and 'God-fearers' were turning to Christ, and the synagogue retaliated by making life very difficult for the Christians; homes and shops were attacked and looted (Rev 13:7; Heb 10:32–34). And there is more to come 'for ten days' (Rev 2:10), a clear reference to Daniel's uncompromising stand in hostile Babylon 'for ten days' (Dan 1:12, 14).

Why won't the Lord step in to save his suffering people and scatter their enemies? One answer is given in the Lord's words:

'As the Father has sent me, I am sending you' (John 20:19–23). Not only are we people sent out with his word for the world, but the manner of our sending is like his. To clinch the principle beyond any shadow of doubt 'he showed them his hands and side'.

Authentic witness to the world will bear the marks of Christ's passion. Our life in the world will be cruciform when it is Christlike. Paul's apostolate was authenticated in the way he was always carrying in his body 'the death of Jesus, so that the life of Jesus may also be manifested in our bodies' (2 Cor 4:7–12). We are not above our Lord in this. His sufferings, those endured by the church at Smyrna and any we may experience as faithful Christians are, says Newbiggin, 'the price paid for a victorious challenge to the powers of evil'. All triumphalism is ruled out by this principle. 'Your king comes to you, gentle and riding on a donkey' (Matt 21:5). The crucified mind speaks there, not the crusading mind. Newbiggin again:

> It is the way the Church must go ... It is a totally uncompromising yet totally vulnerable challenge to the powers of evil in the name and in the power of the kingship of God present in the crucified and risen Jesus ... the authenticating marks of a missionary church will be the marks of the passion – his hands and his side.

The believers at Smyrna are declared 'rich' (Rev 2:9) in the midst of economic suffering. They have weighed up the alternatives and settled for life, new life in Christ and the crown of life beyond the appalling second death (vs 10–11). They were not a recluse community withdrawn into the desert, but townspeople working hard at their daily business. But they chose Christ and said their 'Yes' to eternity, living as though seeing 'him who is invisible' (Heb 11:27). Far from being a fantastic, escapist preoccupation with heaven, openness to God's eternity floods the present with a discerning understanding of our business in this life: 'those who buy something, as if it were not theirs to keep; those who use the things of the world, as if not engrossed in them. For this world in its present form is passing away' (1 Cor 7:29–31).

Not so the secular vision. By definition it can only be claustrophobically enclosed within the visible present. For all their talk about squeezing the last drop of experience out of life, secularists are like children playing in an airless, windowless back room when outside are the glorious forests and mountains. Auden wondered about the poverty of that vision:[5]

Have they ever, one wonders,
Wanted so much to see a unicorn, even
A dead one? Probably. But they won't say so,
Ignoring by tacit consent our hunger
For eternal life, that caged rebuked question...

The marvellous Christians at Smyrna honoured their own hunger for eternal life by their loyalty to the Lord of heaven. In Auden's metaphor, they opened the cage and let their longings for the eternity of God's heaven run free, straight into the arms of their Lord.

Message to Pergamum – battering-rams and airborne germs

Whether it was the courts or the lynch mobs who put Antipas to death, his church kept the faith magnificently 'where Satan has his throne' (Rev 2:13). A rich pluralism of Western and Eastern cults mingled in Pergamum, but the 'Satan's throne' jibe was directed at Rome: Pergamum was the seat of Roman provincial government, an intimidating environment for non-conforming Christians.

A church may courageously withstand the battering-ram of physical or economic persecution, yet be quietly subverted by false teaching. The mobs attack the front door; but false ideas are more like air-borne germs coming up between cracks in the floor boards (vs 14–15, compare Gal 3:1–5). Enter Nicolaitanism.

The teaching of Nicolas of Antioch (Acts 6:5) reminded John of Balaam (Rev 2:14) who was blamed for leading Israel into immorality and participation in pagan cults (Num 25:1–2; 31:16; 2 Peter 2:15–16). We can reasonably guess that the Nicolaitan thing was not a headlong dive into the worst disorders of pagan practices. More probably (and this is where the virus is mightier than the battering-ram) Nicolaitanism proposed a 'sensible' accommodation with the cultural norms that permeated social life, commerce and politics. Thus a Christian could take an easy view of pagan procedures without fear of contamination, since 'All things' are restored to mankind in Christ. Pagan deities and their taboos can be rejected as so much emptiness or benighted superstition from which Jesus has delivered his people. Even the statutory pinch of incense in the flame to Caesar could be construed as harmless enough. No educated Roman believed the emperor to be divine. The imperial cult was really a political mechanism to keep the empire's citizens in line (Caird).

It is a plausible line of reasoning. Paul announced Christian freedom: 'for us there is but one God, the Father, from whom all things came and for whom we live' (1 Cor 8:6). But Caird comments:

> [The] very plausibility of the case (that pagan deities are unreal 'nothings') explains the violent and abusive language John uses to refute it. The pagan gods may not be real gods but that does not mean that they do not exist, that their power is not real power. If the state claims to be divine, though its claim is false, its power is real, the satanic distortion of the genuine authority given to it by God ... if Caesar claims what is due to God alone, this means open war in which there can be no neutrality, a war which is part of the age-long struggle between God and Satan.

If the Ephesian Christians were too judgemental, the Pergamum Christians were too lax. Of the two directions, our Western churches tend towards laxity, living as we do within a complex and powerful pluralism. Trends, ideas, the plausibility of secular dogmas, are communicated with enormous persuasiveness by wall-to-wall media. Whereas Christians like Antipas (Rev 2:13) through the centuries have rejected the false claims of the despots, choosing martyrdom above compromise, modern Christians appear to be surrendering to the seductions of postmodernity with hardly a trace of a struggle. Our minds are being quietly and steadily colonised. For us, the call to 'repent' (vs 5, 16) will require a rediscovery of the truth about Christ who lays claim to everything as his by creation and redemption. 'There is not an inch of any sphere of life of which Jesus Christ the Lord does not say "Mine" ' (Abraham Kuyper).

The 'overcomer' will be the one who rejects the attractive, plausible, soft compromise of pagan banquets (whatever that may mean for you) which are permeated with demonic connotations.

In the lifelong endeavour to overcome (within Christ's decisive overcoming), we become the person God always had in mind for us; called by a new name written on a white stone (v 17). You alone will be able to decipher the ideogram on the stone when you receive it from God, because you alone will have *become* your new name. It is a haunting metaphor of the lifelong and life-making journey of our redemption.

Message to Thyatira – beware the prophetic supernova

Any church which is growing in deeds, love, faith, service and perseverance (v 19) is a glory. Only the 'eyes … like blazing fire' (v 18) could detect something sinister about the leader of the church at Thyatira – a charismatically gifted woman who was in no doubt about her qualities. The criticisms of the 'prophetess' are so similar to those made against the Nicolaitans at Pergamum and Ephesus that we can reasonably assume a connection.

She put John in mind of another powerful woman, Jezebel, who had infuriated Elijah by her efforts to fuse together Baal and Yahweh worship ('syncretism', see 1 Kings 16:31; 21:25; 2 Kings 9:22). The historic Jezebel's 'immorality' was in fact spiritual infidelity (the one is a common biblical metaphor for the other). There lies our clue to the influence of the Thyatiran prophetess: she encouraged harmony between Christ and demons (see 2 Cor 6:14 – 7:1).

We cannot believe that the splendid Thyatiran congregation would embrace blatant Satanism. Something different, more subtle and less obvious is implied by the woman's familiarity with 'Satan's … deep secrets' (Rev 2:24). Possibly her syncretism encouraged unsuspecting Christians to enter as completely as possible into society even though much of it was the acknowledged domain of the demonic. Secure 'in Christ', a believer had his passport to explore even 'Satan's deep secrets' in pagan rituals, and to taste the mystery of evil with impunity, able 'to touch pitch without being defiled and handle fire without being burnt' (Caird). If you think that is too fantastic, look at Paul's strange warning to the Corinthian Christians that 'no-one who is speaking by the Spirit of God says, 'Jesus be cursed' (1 Cor 12:3)! What weird mingling of the Christian and the demonic was going on there?

Or was the prophetess teaching something even more intriguing? That since Christ is Lord over all things, we can ditch this talk about 'them' and 'us', 'enemies' and 'hostile powers'; for Christ is already out there, ahead of us, incognito, dressed in other religions and cultural forms and known by a hundred names, invoked in ancient deities and saviours, celebrated in rituals far older than Christianity? In which case the 'wise' and 'enlightened' believer need struggle no longer to distinguish between religions, but can welcome them all as tributaries flowing into the limitless ocean that is God.

If we are anywhere near the truth about her, then the prophetess translates smoothly into our own time and place. 'This is an age of mix 'em salad-bar spirituality ... where brand loyalty is a doctrine of the past and the customer is king' (*Newsweek*). She is the gnostic mother of syncretism – a fusion, a blurring and a blending of redemption. Syncretism feels right for today: tolerant, broad-minded, worldly-wise, inclusive. It allows messiahs from California and Korea as well as the one from Bethlehem.

The prophetess got away with her line of teaching presumably by claiming inspired prophetic revelations and doing so, no doubt, with style and flair. Unless a congregation knows how to engage with the mind of God by prayerfully listening to him in scripture, they will always be at the mercy of the outpourings of the latest 'prophetic' supernova. This is why the Spirit confers his gifts on the church, so that we might come to wise, discerning judgements (Eph 4:11–16).

The plethora of religions, cults and ways-of-salvation that thrive in society today present us with a tremendous challenge and opportunity. Better this state of affairs by far, surely, than the deadly, grey, atheistic materialism of a few years ago. Certainly there can be no hiding from our world. And the New Testament, speaking as it does out of a far more pluralistic culture than our own, in which Christians were a tiny minority, can show us how to relate to the pluralism in our time.

Paul at Athens offers a superb model (Acts 17:16–34). Entering Athens, he toured the city, looking and listening and finding in their architecture clues to Athenian aspirations. And in their literature: Paul was familiar enough with Athenian poets to be able to select and quote from them in support of his own apologetic (Acts 17:28). Throughout the encounter, his attitude towards the Athenians was courteous and positive. He clearly looked for and expected to discover God's fingerprints on their culture. He found his way into their thinking by means of their shrine to 'The Unknown God'. Yet far from gloating over this token of their agnosticism, he is warmly appreciative of their seriousness (Acts 17:22). It became his text and he expounded it by leading his Athenian listeners on a tour of their own culture (Acts 17:27–29).

We sense that Paul presents himself to the Athenians as a fellow seeker, but one who by the grace of God has come to the Lord they are still in ignorance of. Informed, sensitive, courteous, we feel that here is the crucified mind at work, not the crusading mind. Yet not a hint of compromise and certainly not syncretism. He is unswervingly targeted on Christ as he shares the gospel with the Athenians. Brilliant…

Message to Sardis – less than meets the eye

No mention made here (Rev 3:1–6) of fierce struggles with pagan, imperial or heretical hostilities. No bogus apostles or a maverick prophetess to disturb the peace of the church in Sardis. But it is the quiet of the graveyard (v 1). John analyses their malaise:

A complacent lack of vigilance (vs 2–3)
In fact the Sardis church is following a similar career to that of Sardis city, once a byword for wealth in its pomp under the fabulous King Croesus. It was a prosperous centre of trade and industry, particularly in luxury clothing (v 4, 'dressed in white'), and protected by an almost impregnable fortress-citadel. Yet twice an enemy had penetrated the acropolis – Cyrus in 546BC and Antiochus the Great in 214BC. On both occasions the enemy came not by the usual frontal assault as expected, but by stealth and at night, probing the city's weakest points (v 3, 'like a thief').

Both city and church were resting on former glories and past reputations. Why stay awake on guard all night if there is no danger to be faced? And the apparent absence of opposition to the church in Sardis is worrying. No Christian group should be that bland and inoffensive! Is it that they are too well liked, or are they merely tolerated or simply ignored as irrelevant by local society? Where is the struggle, the perspiration, the striving after the new name on their white stone?

Contrast the urgent tension of Charles Wesley's prayer:[6]

> To serve the present age,
> My calling to fulfill –
> O may it all my powers engage
> To do my master's will!
>
> Arm me with jealous care,
> As in thy sight to live,
> And O thy servant, Lord, prepare
> A strict account to give.

The stained garments (v 4)

Since the white robe is an image of the sinner's justification by the blood of Christ (7:14), the soiled robe implies some compromise over the cross. It figures – the cross compels choice. All are judged before it, and all other forms of redemption are declared impotent to reach and heal our fundamental disorders. The cross is bound to place the one who trusts in it out of kilter with others who reject it (Gal 6:14). T S Eliot was right to argue that 'it is the church's business to interfere with the world'. No sign of that between the church and the city at Sardis. These Christians were not prepared to allow the cross to cause them any embarrassment with their neighbours.

They carry nothing through to fulfilment

This is the blunt meaning of the remark, 'I have not found your deeds complete' (Rev 3:2). Content with their mediocrity, this bland innocuous congregation lacks the drive to take on real projects for the kingdom of God and see them through to completion, whatever the cost. They have no tenacity in the things of God. 'There are many who dare not kill themselves for fear of what the neighbours will say' runs a proverb, which suits rather well the vapid Sardis church. They are tasteless salt, good for nothing. Worse than nothing because when God's people fail to embody the gospel authentically, they become 'a nearly indispensable midwife to the birth of our boring, one-dimensional culture'.

Yet even for this moribund church there is an astonishing chance of life. The Lord who will, if need be, burst in upon them in judgement 'like a thief' (v 3), comes first with 'the seven spirits of God' (v 1), indicating the Holy Spirit in the complete fullness (seven) of his power and gifts. People touched by the Holy Spirit become filled with a holy restlessness and innovative energy. They dream and see visions of the world where God works his newness against all reason and in the face of the most unpromising circumstances. Ireland's great missionary, Patrick, described his own experience: 'I used to be roused to prayer in snow and in frost and rain, and I felt no harm, nor was there any inclination to take things easily in me because, as I see now, the Spirit seethed in me'.

Imagine the Sardis church baptised in the seething Holy Spirit and participating in God's holy discontent within Sardis city. A church renewed in the seething Spirit will 'bear small but highly combustible seeds of God's imagination'. Now that would be a church worth persecuting!

For God's sake do something courageous!
(Zwingli)

Message to Philadelphia – the power of a little strength

How can we measure the quality of a church? The Gospels are clear – stop counting and start weighing. As a measure of what was real and true in his life, Augustine decided 'my love is my weight'. On that scale the Philadelphians rate highly, although they are said to be of 'little strength' (v 8), 'little' probably meaning size. In terms of their status and clout in Philadelphia, they were certainly 'little'. But these Christians loved God: 'you have kept my word and have not denied my name … you have kept my command to endure patiently' (vs 8, 10). We get the impression not so much of a fizzing congregation as one with deep integrity. When people of 'little strength' are well connected to the Lord, they become a potent force for his purposes. Scripture delights in examples: Abraham, Noah, Gideon, David (against Goliath) and Daniel.

A small, embattled group jeopardised by the synagogues' hostility (v 9) would naturally tend to turn in on itself and huddle together for mutual support. But God will have none of it: 'I have placed before you an open door' (v 8). Mission, not maintenance. Expansion, not the management of decline (Acts 14:27; 1 Cor 16:9; 2 Cor 2:12; Col 4:3). God is at work, moving, disturbing, revealing, opening doors for his witnessing people to enter. The Holy Spirit is able to enter hearts and minds, and unlock doors and shutters from within. He enters where we have no power or authority to enter (which is why we should reject any human tinkering around on the inside of people's minds to bring about a decision).

Jesus is still the evangelist, teacher and healer. As in the days of his incarnation, so now he is at work up and down our world and in the streets of our neighbourhoods, searching out 'the scattered children of God, to bring them together and make them one' (John 11:51–52). Our part is to keep close behind him as he directs his people into fruitful encounters with men and women. 'Let your nets down here' – within that relationship 'little strength' is taken up into the mighty purposes of God. Similarly with the matter of our faith. It is not great quantities of faith that are necessarily required; faith as small as a mustard seed will do if it is connected with the activities of the Spirit. This will be enough to bring us into the gravitational pull of the divine mission and we will 'move mountains' (Luke 17:5–6). It is a partnership, of sorts, as in the African proverb about the elephant and the flea who walked hand in hand over a wooden bridge. On the other side the flea looked back and said, 'My, we certainly gave *that* a shaking'.

Augustine expressed the same truth: 'Without God we cannot – Without us he will not'. The implications of this principle for our peace of mind are enormous. For one thing, it means we will go about our daily business, praying to discern the open doors or those left on the latch by the Lord. This is more satisfactory than butting our heads against doors that are barred and bolted. And it lifts the burden of false, pseudo-responsibilities, when we act as if everything depends on us. We do tend to take ourselves far too seriously in mission, because we forget our place – we really are the flea in this partnership. Christ leads and prepares the ground: we enter as we follow and participate in his activity; we overcome within his overcoming. Thus we are released from the burden of playing the Messiah, to undertake joyfully our real responsibilities.

But the opportunities are not perpetually there; the same door is not held open indefinitely. The door is open *now*. Enter into the Lord's purposes *now*. The key word is *kairos*, the New Testament word for time seen as timing, timeliness, the right moment. As when the milk in the saucepan comes to the boil and *now* it is ready. As in our Lord's analogy of weather forecasting, where he asks how it is that we are skilled at reading and interpreting the sky but 'don't know how to interpret this present time' (Luke 12:54–56). The opportunities will soon pass (or change), with the onset of persecution, that 'hour of trial' (Rev 3:10). Yet in God's hands even these grim events can become another *kairos* moment.

Thus the Lord pays the Philadelphians a tremendous compliment. He believes that they are alert and flexible enough to respond to the open door of opportunity, that they are not boxed into a rigid, self-perpetuating church programme. They need to be firm and grounded at the centre (vs 8, 10), but fluid and inventive on the periphery where they touch the local Philadelphian world.

Persecution is coming (v 10): so too is the Lord Jesus (v 11). Is that strange? We believe his promise, 'I am with you always' (Matt 28:20). Yet here he says, 'I am coming soon.' How can the Lord, who is already here, come? He is indeed present with his people, but not in a static, uniform way like the fixed pattern on the wallpaper or the constant unchanging presence of the air we breath. He is not with us as an unvarying background presence. He comes, and is always ready to come, in a particular capacity, to minister to us in an appropriate way.

In fact, we do practice both his presence and his coming. We practice his presence by giving thanks continually for every aspect of daily life, by blessing God, saying those simple 'thank yous' which routinely express our conviction that the Lord is here. In this way we cultivate an awareness of the presence of God and of life's holy potential; by blessing God for all things we drive back the encroaching secular wasteland:

> The desert and the parched land will be glad;
> the wilderness will rejoice and blossom.
>
> (Isaiah 35:1)

We practice his coming by expecting it to happen daily under cover of ordinary events, the duties and joys, which the saints have called 'the Sacrament of the Present Moment'. Eternity is spliced into present time; heaven hovers around everyday life. The Lord speaks out of the storm (Job 38:1) and in 'the soft, barely audible sound of almost breathing' (1 Kings 19:11–12). Anything can be a channel of his coming, everything can speak of his presence. It is a vision of our life in the present which constantly opens up towards the coming of the city of God and of our Lord Jesus in his final 'coming again' (Rev 3:12).

The lesson of Philadelphia is plain: eyes off our 'little strength' and onto our mighty Lord who is always here and always coming:[7]

> Blessed are you, Sovereign God of all,
> To you be glory and praise for ever!
> As we look for your coming among us this day,
> Open our eyes to behold your presence
> And strengthen our hands to do your will,
> That the world may rejoice and give you praise,
> Father, Son and Holy Spirit. Amen.

Message to Laodicea – where is the fire?

The realism of the seven letters is disturbing: we recognise ourselves in the shortcomings of those first Christians. But we are also reassured. The Lord worked newness in them: he can do the same in us.

The church in Laodicea was a well-heeled church in an affluent society. The city was a banking and commercial centre, with a flourishing textile industry and a medical school well-known for its eye and ear medications. Money, wool and pharmaceuticals: John will play on these features of Laodicean prosperity (Rev 3:17–18).

We have noted in the other letters that John saw the local church as coloured by its location. Of course – we are all children of our place and time, and continue to be so after conversion. Our culture shapes the voice with which we answer Christ's call. We have no other voice. Conversion must include and convert the cultural expressions of our lives too. We are to bring them, in all their complex layers and textures, their signs, languages and attitudes, to be baptised into Jesus Christ and for his service. The cultural voice we have requires the fullest, richest possible range of tone and colour and knowledge. It includes everything that is capable of being consecrated. The challenge for us is 'to plunder the Egyptians without setting up the Golden Calf', and this is where the Laodiceans failed miserably.

Affluence is a wonderful blessing, but it has potentially hazardous consequences for faith unless we act to bring our wealth under Christ's Lordship. If not, then the by-products of wealth – security, independence, power, status and self-image – will certainly draw our gaze away from God and down to his goods, from the Giver to his gifts. The result is Laodicean apathy: commitment, sacrificial discipleship, zeal and the high risk of love are overwhelmed by complacency and mediocrity.

The Laodiceans will wonder what all the fuss is about. Why go to such lengths to seek after God with every fibre of one's being, as if one's very existence depended upon it, when obviously all is well and 'I am rich; I have acquired wealth and do not need a thing' (v 17)?

The result is an ethos that is neither one thing nor the other. The Laodiceans lack the spiritual energy to come out clearly for God (or the devil) and probably would not see the point of doing so. Spiritually shallow, half-hearted, they are incapable of anything as bold as full-blooded heresy: they are 'lukewarm'.

The Laodicean condition describes 'nominalism'. There are

many reasons why nominal Christians bother with the faith, but a passionate desire to know God with every ounce of their being is not one of them. The nominal Christian is puzzled and embarrassed by high spiritual commitment. Enthusiasm (in its original sense of being God-possessed, God-inspired) is looked upon as definitely dangerous, too direct, far too 'in your face'. After visiting a Laodicean-type congregation in Norwich, John Wesley remarked, 'How can it be thought that the old coarse Gospel should find admission there?'

Christ's protest against the nauseating Laodiceans reveals him to be on the side of the extremists: extreme in his love, extreme in the lengths to which he will go to redeem his world by the cross, extreme in his new covenant commitment to his people. Of all things, an extremist cannot stomach cool indifference, the absence of passion and perspiration. What were they like, the preachers at Laodicea? Martin Luther described their ilk as delivering the sort of preaching which 'couldn't persuade a dog out from behind a warm stove'. God is disgusted by safe, vapid, passionless Laodiceanism.

G K Chesterton lampooned this Laodicean mentality as a feature of our own times – the inability to make large, heroic, outrageous decisions and to stick to them:[8]

> The man who makes a vow makes an appointment with himself at some distant time or place ... [but] a modern man refrains from swearing to count the leaves on every third tree in Holland Walk, not because it is silly to do so (he does many sillier things) but because he has a profound conviction that before he has got to the three hundred and seventy-ninth leaf on the first tree, he would be excessively tired of the subject and want to go home to tea ... And this is the condition of the decadent. To be everlastingly passing through dangers which we know cannot scathe us, to be taking oaths which we know cannot bind us, to be defying enemies who we know cannot conquer us – this is the grinning tyranny of decadence which is called freedom ... thus they say, 'Let us have the pleasures of conquerors without the pains of soldiers: let us sit on

sofas and be a hardy race ... Let us have the splendour of
offering ourselves without the peril of committing ourselves; let us see whether one cannot commit suicide an
unlimited number of times'.

As the Laodicean experience demonstrates, affluence can leave us
in a state of self-delusion – material well-being is taken to indicate a satisfactory spiritual condition. A wretched, pitiful, poor,
blind, naked man who believes that things could not be better is,
we might think, just about beyond redemption. Our hope is in the
severe mercies of the love of God (3:19). First, a swift diagnosis
delivered without a trace of sugar: 'You say ... but you are' (v 17),
as if the doctor should announce, 'I've seen your X-rays and I
have to tell you...' Followed by equally unambiguous, urgent
direction: 'buy from me' (v 18). Healing will come by a radical
relocation of our lives away from these sterile centres (person-
centred, things-centred, power-centred, me-centred) and onto the
one centre of life – Jesus Christ, the 'Amen' (v 14). The root idea
in that word is strong, steadfast, consistent purpose. And 'Amen'
is a liturgical response, the 'Yes' to God's promises and invitation.
Christ is that clinching 'Yes – Amen' to God's creative and re-cre-
ative work in the world and in the church. The sum total of the
incarnation is called 'the faithful and true witness', his 'Yes' in his
living and dying to the way God is redeeming the world.

As 'the ruler [the beginning, the origin, the ultimate source] of
God's creation' (v 14) Jesus shoulders the yoke of the Father's
purposes. He has hitched himself to the cart of God's kingdom to
bring all things through to perfection: 'Buy from *me*.'

> For no matter how many promises God has made, they are
> 'Yes' in Christ. And so through him the 'Amen' is spoken
> by us to the glory of God.
>
> (2 Corinthians 1:20)

Christ brings his resources to act upon the Laodiceans: 'Here I am!
I stand at the door and knock' (Rev 3:20). This divine courtesy and
condescension are astonishing when he knocks and calls. Anything
can act for him. As we shall see later in Revelation, at the mega-
level Christ can knock for entry into the heart of a society – by

political upheaval, natural disaster and crisis. At the personal and congregational level he can use those 'pigsty' moments of personal trauma and the wonderful 'champagne' moments of great joy. They are saying, 'Here I am! Where are you?' These encounters, too, have a *kairos* dimension. They are moments of opportunity for reconciliation and renewal, *now,* while he knocks.

Open your heart and Christ will enter. Even this action, seemingly of our own volition, is due to his initiatives, for the saints have always known that God first gives what God commands. He enters, and at once we are sharing a meal together. In the culture of the Gospels, a meal is always the sign of reconciliation. Old feuds are finished, debts are wiped off; together we make a fresh start. This meal (v 20) signifies the fundamental transaction of renewal: as Christ is given access to our hearts, so he gives us access to himself and his resources. Each time we share the bread and wine at Communion we enact this truth.

Finally, the Overcomer

At last it is possible to see what John has been getting at with his 'overcomer' refrain at the conclusion of each of the seven messages (v 21). Everything written in the letters is with the practical purpose of encouraging an 'overcoming' quality of faith. This was the reason for the new apocalypse (unveiling or revelation) of Jesus Christ. To each local church, in its own unique set of circumstances, the living Lord has been introduced by aspects of his vision that match their particular local circumstances. The resources of the risen Lord are targeted, and applied personally and locally. The corollary of this measured appropriateness is that each local congregation can indeed overcome by the power of Christ's overcoming, in terms of its real 'bricks and mortar' locality: that is, not overcoming in general, or in principle, or in a universal sense, but among the noises and sights and people and circumstances of where each one lives. The Apocalypse is for the whole church at all times, and for my church on the corner of my street.

CRITICAL HEIGHT

Revelation 4

While we are left to ourselves, embedded as we are in the present moment, we are unable to see 'what is now and what will take place later' (1:19). We are like a man standing so close to a brick wall that he cannot tell if the building is a cathedral or an abattoir. We must have some critical distance from, and height above, the present order if we are to see what is going on. This is why we follow John through that door and up into his visionary heaven.

We are standing in what appears to be part temple and part military command centre at Supreme HQ. Around us move signs, symbols, people, creatures, lights. They are apocalyptic indicators of the state of the warfare taking place on earth between heaven and hell. Over everything and dominating the entire scene is the throne of God (4:2), indicating that whatever the ebb and flow of the conflict, its outcome is already decided. This is a genuine battle, with real consequences for winners and losers, but from first to last the divine sovereignty dominates. From this height, from the perspective of the throne, we are able to see the unfolding of history while, at the same time, we look past history to its consummation. We have the critical height of prophetic perspective which is the special gift of Revelation.

Picture the indescribable

John attempts no description of the One who occupies the throne. Each phrase and metaphor merely deepens the sense of the numinous, incomprehensible mystery – uncanny strangeness added to indescribable wonder, 'jasper, carnelian ... emerald'. The glory of God bathes heaven in incandescent radiance. Language peters out, description is exhausted; the scene appears quarried out of ecstatic fire, 'teasing imagination out of all thought'.

An ordinary mortal could not survive the burning purity of this place – like falling into the sun – except for 'a rainbow ... encircling the throne' (v 3). Keep your eye on that rainbow as you approach the throne. It is the covenant sign given to Noah (Gen 9:12–17) which adds grace and mercy to every other attribute of the Almighty. The light-refracting throne projects the spectrum of grace over and around God's every word and action (Heb 4:16), even, dare we say it, making the throne 'the place of our sanctuary' (Jer 17:12), our familiar home.

Even so, a man cannot stare straight at God and remain alive: this principle traverses scripture (Exod 19:21; 33:20). God becomes a reality for us when we learn to look at him, as it were, out of the corner of our eye, as his unbearable light is refracted through those people to whom God is everything. Even in heaven it seems this is so, until the final transformation takes place in us and we 'will see his face' (Rev 22:4).

Pointing to the central majesty

Here are people, creatures, and even inanimate creation, all of which have been profoundly affected by the grace of God. They attract our gaze by their strange otherness. Because they are oriented towards the throne, they draw our eyes that way also. They are witnesses pointing away to the central majesty.

We see *twenty-four elders* (4:4): twelve patriarchal heads of Israel's tribes plus the twelve apostles. Together they represent the entire host of the overcoming people of God. They are called 'a kingdom and priests to serve [Christ's] God and Father' (1:6). This is how we may live before the throne and bear the light of the All-Holy One upon our spirits, even to explore the vision – by a reverent and adoring mind, and in the humility of worship:

> What I know of thee I bless,
> As acknowledging thy stress
> On my being, and as seeing
> Something of thy holiness.
>   (Gerard Manley Hopkins)[1]

Ben Sirach also expresses well the experience of trying to worship adequately, that is, trying to keep up with the runaway beauty of God:

> When you praise the Lord, exalt him as much as you can;
> for he will surpass even that. When you exalt him, put
> forth all your strength, and do not grow weary, for you
> cannot praise him enough. Who has seen him and can
> describe him? Or who can extol him as he is?

There is a suggestion here that striving to do justice to God in our praise is not a question of problem solving, like doing difficult mental arithmetic, but like a delightful game or art in which we will grow all the more accomplished by the doing of it.

> Wherefore with my utmost art I will sing thee,
> And the cream of all my heart I will bring thee.
>   (George Herbert)[2]

Before the throne there is *a sea of glass*, 'clear as crystal' (4:6). It was not always so. Generally the Old Testament people hated the sea: 'the wicked are like the tossing sea, which cannot rest, whose waves cast up mire and mud' (Isaiah 57:20). In Daniel the sea is the heaving reservoir of human evil in the heart of the nations, the spawning ground of his four terrible creatures, all teeth and claws, – symbols of the four great empires of the ancient world (Dan 7:2–7). Those particular beasts have disappeared but the sea continues to produce others (Rev 13:1) – monstrous powers, tyrants and their systems, Caesars, Hitlers, Stalins and Pol Pots. Yet in John's vision the sea has undergone total transformation: it is drained of evil, transparent, serene, mirroring the beauty of God's holiness at the consummation of cosmic redemption.

The mysterious *four living creatures* (4:6–9) appear to represent the whole created cosmos of earth and heaven. Clearly they are related to the cherubim who support the cosmic throne in Ezekiel's vision (Ezek 1:4–21) and also to Isaiah's seraphim who stand before the throne of God (Isaiah 6:2). Their work, in the ancient visions and in this heaven, is the same: to orchestrate adoration for the All Holy One (Rev 4:8–9), 'weaving plainsong into a garland' (vs 10–11).

Anxiety and the throne

These awesome 'pointers to the central majesty' all have a cosmic reference. Yet we are ourselves, in our individual lives, part of that reality. Therefore we are right to ask what effect the presence of the throne of God might have on the people we are. Indeed, how will a sceptical world see evidence of God's day-to-day sovereignty unless, as his witnesses, his people mirror something of it? The presence of the throne in our affairs should make all the difference; otherwise it will appear to be merely so much triumphalist Christian rhetoric.

Let us be straightforward about this question and imagine John's state of mind at the time of his visions. He was aware of the impending suffering for his congregations on the mainland. He would – not to exaggerate – be prone to anxiety for them. He brought that anxiety with him before the throne.

Anxiety. A nationwide poll among young people in Germany included the question, 'What is the basic feeling you have toward life?' Sixty per cent replied, 'Fear.' Not fear of death but fear of life. 'Anxiety' would be a more exact description of the emotion reported in the poll, because their fear was about the future. Anxiety is the irrational and uncontrollable response to our dread of the unknown. Like gas, however small the amount, it will always expand to occupy all the available space.

The reality of the throne has the greatest relevance to our anxieties. Can it possibly be the will of God that our inner world be distressed by the dark, steady misery of anxiety about the possible harm waiting to leap out from an unknown future? No. 'God threatens terrible things if we will not be happy' (Jeremy Taylor), which rather turns the tables on anxiety. The throne is the almighty power standing behind Taylor's startling remark. And the throne energises Lady Julian's well-known promise that 'all will be well – and all will be well – and all manner of thing will be well', an infuriatingly naïve sentiment if it were not for the fact of the throne and its rainbow. These lines from an old hymn are even more precise about why we can go free of anxiety:

I know not what the future holds
But I know who holds the future.

The future belongs to God, the Alpha and the Omega, and 'all the demons we meet have been already doomed and damned by the Christ who ruined them' (P T Forsyth). Should we go in fear of doomed, damned, ruined demons?

If more were needed to exorcise anxiety, surely John himself has supplied it: 'perfect love drives out fear' (1 John 4:18). Not our perfect love, of course, but God's love which is able to perfectly fulfil in us what he, in love, perfectly imagines. In Christ God has done everything necessary to expel worry and fear, and to possess our imaginations with his healing *shalom*. The characteristic effect of his deliverance from the tyranny of anxiety is laughter.

Patrick Kavanagh called Christ's resurrection, 'A laugh freed for ever and ever'. And the psalmist wrote: 'The One enthroned in heaven laughs' (Psalm 2:4), going on to give the reason for the divine rejoicing: 'I have installed my King' (Psalm 2:6). Laughter in the presence of the anxious can be cruel provocation. Or it may offer temporary respite, a brief forgetting, drowning out the nag of anxiety with a few laughs before returning to prison as though nothing has changed. But Christ's Easter laughter from the throne explodes under the prison door:

> ...neither death nor life, neither angels nor demons [nor worry, fear, anxiety], neither the present nor the future, nor any powers, neither height nor depth, nor anything else in all creation, will be able to separate us from the love of God that is in Christ Jesus our Lord.
>
> (Romans 8:38–39)

Which is not to conjure up a fantasy about a life without trials and challenges. Rather it is about courageous, self-forgetful, joyful living.

> Our whole life is continually thrown into the air in praise in the trust that it will be caught, blessed and returned renewed.[3]

THE SCROLL AND THE LAMB

Revelation 5

Even as John stood in heaven celebrating God's good government, hostile authorities were targeting his churches. God reigns, but how does he reign?

We must stay at the throne for our answers. Any attempt to reason our way into the truth, with our backs turned to God, will end only in disappointment. No one can establish the actions of God objectively. Earthquakes do not come labelled 'This one is (or isn't) from God.' To interpret the mystery and message of God's activities, we place ourselves entirely in his hands. Therefore, *we believe in order to understand.* We must know the judge in order to understand his judgements. All eyes are on a scroll (v 1).

The scroll: suspicion or submission?

We are saying that the scroll contains the world's destiny. It is held in God's right hand to signify that it is his, foreordained in his absolute love and infinite wisdom. This is not to suggest that everything that emerges from the scroll will be sweetness and light. But this vision implies that, whatever appears, it must pass through God's hands and is under his control, including the fact of John's hostile authorities. The scroll is in God's right hand, therefore we know that nothing can escape his active and personal government as he moves in our affairs.

Our secularist friends find this idea an intolerable intrusion into their personal freedom to pursue their own lives as they see fit. For them it smacks of the trammels and burdens laid on the human race by religion since the start of history. We can say two things in reply to this criticism.

First, how do they understand 'freedom'? This problem is as old as Adam. Satan whispered in Adam's ear the slander that is deeply embedded in the natural mind: God is really just a great spoilsport, the soul's hangman, forever finding ways to hold us down and check our enjoyment, even a little threatened by our brilliant independence (Gen 3:4–5). It is a scandal that Christians have too often lived their faith as though it were a limited, puny and pious thing, thereby adding weight to that ancient lie.

Believers who know differently despair at this grotesque misrepresentation. We know a God 'whose service is perfect freedom'. And this is the key – freedom and joy in God for those who let him have his way. It is freedom via the strait gate and the narrow way of the disciplines of life in the kingdom of God (Matt 7:13–14). Discipline, as when the acorn is released to grow true to its nature into a majestic oak. We really do not want our acorns claiming their independence to grow into, say, a rice pudding. We would call that many things but certainly not freedom.

The freedom that comes from allowing God to be God is something like the freedom in dancing. The music releases and the music controls. The dancer submits to the music, goes with it, and is thereby released within it. Her skill lies in her ability to interpret and innovate within the limits of the music. The music lets the dancer go, and the music holds her. No wonder the first Christians in their catacomb art portrayed Christ as Orpheus, the fabulous music-maker who could charm the wild animals out of the forest. Charmed by the will of God is a fine way of describing it: the Lord is our control and he is our release. As poet Michael O'Siadhail writes of a piece of music:[1]

A pose not a posture; no truculent stance
Toys here with despair. The word is praise,
The theme a scale of infinite permutation.

The second question we have for our friends who reject the idea of the destiny-scroll in the hand of God is this: how goes it in your brave new world independent of divine interference?

To take just one indicator, look at the children. The first comprehensive children's health survey compiled by the Office of Population Censuses and Survey reveals the following: infant and child mortality rates in the United Kingdom have halved since 1971. Children are taller, heavier, have better teeth and suffer fewer infectious diseases. But then come the worrying signs. Children are healthier but more miserable. One in five suffers psychiatric disturbance. There is increasing 'psychosocial disorder': moderate or severe behaviour problems affect 7 per cent of inner-city three-year-olds. Harmful forms of behaviour, such as smoking, drinking, drug-taking, are proving difficult to discourage. And, most alarming of all, the number of boys in the 15–19 age range who commit suicide has increased by 45 per cent (by 24 per cent among girls). Obviously, socioeconomic factors impact on these figures. But if children are the best clue to the well-being of a society, our own seems to be in the throes of a nervous breakdown.

Technically brilliant, we are spiritually chaotic and morally all over the place. Poet Kathleen Raine, in her poem 'Loss of Memory', believes we have abandoned our children (and it started back in the Sixties, if not earlier) to a spiritual amnesia, ignorance of the word of God. They are sent out into this strange culture of ours not knowing 'Our Father in Heaven', or the healing words 'Let not your heart be troubled', or the shepherd who can lead into green pastures by the still waters, or 'the twelve signs of love, that never fails' (1 Cor 13). At the end of this disenchanted and murderous century, and in spite of its technical splendour, Christians can feel affirmed in their conviction that it is best to stay with the Maker's instructions.

> God's plans for us are close, not loose, they fit us like a glove; for the thought of God goes with our every motion, divine care clothes us like the atmosphere. And yet, his thought for us does not constrain us; what he designs for us is that we should freely act; what he creates is liberty. To enter into God's plans for us is to be most sovereignly ourselves … We cannot escape from God; but then we do not want to; for why? We should cease to breathe.
>
> (Austin Farrer)[2]

Which suggests that the problem with our God-rejecting culture is that it is starved of oxygen, claustrophobic, gasping for air. The purposes of God as they flow from the throne are the world's oxygen. Which brings us to the puzzle of the scroll, sealed up tight.

The scroll: dangerous if unopened

The appeal for a qualified scroll-opener is unanswered (Rev 5:2–3). What is the problem? What is to prevent God himself from unsealing it? This question goes to the heart of the way in which God rules. He is our Father, not our programmer. We are his children, not pieces on his chess board. He brings humankind into being for a partnership grounded in mutual love and delight. The scroll is about humankind, and it is for human beings to take it and make it their own story. The rabbis said, 'Everything is in the power of God except the love of God.' The scroll awaits one from the human race, who is truly one of us, who, through love, will take it from the Father's hand. God cannot actually compel this move. He cannot command humanity into a partnership of love. In this sense, dare we say, he is vulnerable, like a lover who can call, invite, woo, but not coerce.

There are no qualified scroll-takers; no one who, as a human being and on behalf of the rest of us, can master the secrets of the scroll by his own complete agreement to the divine purposes, and then mediate them to our race.

Heaven falls silent. John is appalled at the implications of this silence (v 4). If the destiny-scroll remains unopened, unknown, unseen, sealed up and confined to heaven, then a nightmare gap opens up between the governing throne and the earth. Demonic or lunatic powers may invade the empty space and work their mischief on the world (Eph 2:2). Unless the gracious purposes of God are able to exert their influence on the world's affairs and so connect heaven and earth, we will be left to the mercy of our chaos.

Images transposed: the lion-lamb

The silence is broken. John can breath again; heaven explodes with praise. There is an answer, one answer: Jesus Christ. But his description is extraordinary even by Revelation's standards of imagery. First, John hears of a lion – majestic, implacable, powerful, unapproachable (Rev 5:5): Christ has returned from his mission, leaving the satanic powers shattered in his wake. The Overcomer, he has destroyed everything that would negate God's purpose. He is qualified to take and open the scroll.

Thus far, the lion image suggests omnipotence flowing out as naked force and irresistible coercion. But when John turns to look at the one who is like a lion, he sees one who is like a lamb still bearing the marks of its slaughter (v 6). How do we reconcile this surreal juxtaposition of opposite images? The slain lamb is, of course, the symbol of the crucified Christ, 'the Lamb of God, who takes away the sin of the world' (John 1:29). The 'power' of the powerless, defenceless man pinned to the cross is that his sin-bearing and atoning death took all our offences and also nailed them to his cross: 'having disarmed the powers and authorities, he made a public spectacle of them, triumphing over them by the cross' (Col 2:14–15). The power of the lion was let loose against God's (and our) enemies in the form of the lamb.

The two images taken together redefine omnipotence: Almighty power (the lion) limitless in its self-giving, seeking, persuading love (the lamb). When you pray for the power of God to do this or that thing, are you thinking of sheer, naked power or the omnipotence of love?

That the leading image of the two is Christ as the lamb is clear (Rev 5:6): the lamb's seven horns (complete power) and seven eyes (infinite wisdom) are applied in the world by the seven spirits (the fullness of the Holy Spirit). As the slain lamb, Christ is qualified to come to the throne, to take and open the scroll! (v 7); as the lamb he is adored in ecstatic praise by those who see and understand these things far better than we can (vs 8–14).

Delighting in the upside down

The lion who is in fact a lamb is a wonderful instance of the way the Lord loves to stand our usual arrangements on their head, of our upside-down faith. We talk of the wisdom of foolishness, the wolf with the lamb, the last who are first, the little child who leads, he who keeps his life losing it, those who have being given more, the power of cross, and the lamb on the throne. Someone has termed these inversions God's 'jazz factor' because (as in jazz) he endlessly innovates and invents with the great theme of his everlasting love for men and women. Surely it is not difficult to hear that irrepressible Easter laughter around the throne for the lamb who is the lion.

THE SEALS

Revelation 6

Christ reigns, qualified in every respect to release the scroll; his
people cry 'Amen' (5:14). But unless Christ's Lordship extends
into our world of hard facts he remains a figurehead only. So the
cry now is 'Come!' (6:1), for we long for his kingly power, which
is celebrated with such ecstasy in the invisible world, to penetrate
and command affairs in this world. 'Come!' Lord Jesus, let your
kingly purposes prevail on earth as they do in heaven.

'Amen – Come' holds in tension the glory and the struggle of
our Christian experience. The glory puts the struggle in perspective. But struggle there most certainly is. During the last thirty-
five years of his life John witnessed events that put a real question
mark against heaven's 'Amen': earthquakes in AD60; the fire in
Rome in AD64 which provoked the persecution of Christians; the
bitter four-year Jewish war that left Jerusalem in ruins in AD70;
the political and military chaos following Nero's suicide in AD68;
the terrifying eruption of Vesuvius in AD79 which created such
darkness that people feared the end of the world had come; and,
in AD92, the grain famine. How does the reign of Christ relate to
such happenings? What is there in the destiny-scroll to assure a
bewildered world, and John's churches in particular, that God is
in control of history?

There are seven seals on the scroll. Seven is the number of
completeness and perfection (see pp 7–9). We therefore take the
sevenfold visions of the seals – and later the trumpets and the
bowls – to refer to the entire present age, from Christ's ascension
until his return at the end of time. With this interpretation, at anytime, anywhere in the world, discerning people will see or hear
the opening of seals, trumpet blasts of warning, or a bowl of the
divine wrath poured out onto the earth.

The four horsemen

Christ opens the first four seals (6:1–8). We are agog to see just how God will exert his authority in history. Not unreasonably, we would expect some sign of his redeeming love to step out of the scroll: angelic forces of light, perhaps, or a battalion of miracle workers. In fact four horsemen ride out. We recognise them immediately since they appear regularly on our television newscasts. The rider on the white horse is Conquest (v 2), the rider on the red horse is Rebellion (v 4), black represents Famine (v 5), and the rider on the pale horse is Plague (v 8; see Zech 6:5–7).

Calling them out of the scroll is not the same as calling them into existence. God does not invent these awful afflictions for the human race. They are nobody's responsibility but our own; they are, said Jesus, of our own creation (Mark 7:20–23), and have been riding the earth since Adam left Eden. They are as old as cruelty, pride and human greed. The first horseman provides employment for the second, the second for the third, and so on. Thus in any of the recent major conflicts – as in Rwanda and Uganda or Bosnia – attack, slaughter and conquest give rise to famine which leads inexorably to disease in a weakened populace, whether they are still at liberty, or in refugee or prison camps. The four horsemen are symbols of John's real world as they are of our own.

The master of paradox

The four horsemen are not willed by God but tolerated and allowed to exist by his permission while remaining restrained by Christ's leash ('a quarter of the earth' only, Rev 6:8). Thus God allows the world its space and freedom to go on being the world, in the hope that men and women and their governments will not abuse his incredible patience and love, but will read the signs, turn and seek the Lord while there is time.

The fact that terrible things emerge from the destiny-scroll in Christ's hands signifies that nothing, not even intrinsically evil things, can escape his control or occur outside his permission. Not even the dire consequences of man's cruelty towards man as symbolised by the four horsemen. Nothing can set up shop independent of God's authority.

If this seems a very hard doctrine to accept, consider the alternative: that evil powers could occupy territory (my territory?) beyond God's reach or influence. Isaiah gave the definitive statement of this truth in the most uncompromising terms so that no one should misunderstand:

> I form the light and create darkness,
>> I bring prosperity and create disaster;
> I, the Lord, do all these things.
>> (Isaiah 45:7)

The context of Isaiah's statement is instructive. God is using the King Cyrus of Persia to liberate his people (Isaiah 45:1). An astounding idea for Israel, that God should call a pagan leader his 'anointed'. Cyrus, of course, is simply doing what a powerful military commander in the ascendancy would do, attacking and destroying Israel's Babylonian captors. But Cyrus' free-will decision to go to war ends up serving the gracious purposes of God whose hand is inside the glove of political movements. Thus 'darkness' and 'disaster' are both man's work, but exist with God's permission and (this is the point) are made to serve his redeeming plans. Thus God 'brings prosperity' – *shalom* – out of the whole man-made mess. That is how he both allows the world its freedom and governs it.

This mysterious principle was raised to its highest power at the cross. Human evil expressed through politics, religion and culture, and infiltrated by the spiritual powers of darkness, exerted its full might to drive Christ out of the world by crucifying him. The people concerned were allowed, within the divine permission, to pursue their schemes. It was truly *their* desire and plan, *their* dreadful choice and action, but in the end they succeeded only in producing a saviour for humankind!

It is therefore in the most paradoxical of John's images – the slain lamb at the throne of God – that Christ opens the scroll, allowing the horsemen to pass through his hands into human experience. Our Lord Jesus is the master of this paradox, that evil is allowed to rampage only to be completely outwitted and outmanoeuvred by God's almighty love and harnessed to serve his purposes.

The unbeliever will see only the suffering of war and famine, and think it can be fully explained in terms of political processes without any need to bring the deity into it. Indeed, the unbeliever, observing the chaos and outraged at the hurts inflicted on so many innocent people, may scorn the Christian's belief in divine judgement acting in human affairs. He makes the mistake of equating God's permission with the absence or non-existence of a God of love. It leaves him either with a false sense of security in relation to God, or at the mercy of his personal despair at what seems to be a human race more than a touch deranged, and history 'a tale told by an idiot'.

Choices

Christ opens seals five and six (Rev 6:9–17). The fifth seal reveals that the church is required to be patient and 'wait a little longer' (vs 9–11) until Christ's overcoming victory is finally won again in each of his pilgrim people. The final accounting is not yet. Christians must continue to live as 'resident aliens' among people of earthbound vision who cannot understand their passion for travel (Heb 11:13–16; 13:14). Both cannot be right. Either 'home' is in the here and now, comfortably settled within the limits of the world; or it actually is ahead and beyond. Choices must be made and they carry the greatest possible significance for our lives; which brings the sixth seal (Rev 6:12–17).

Scenes of global and cosmic disturbance like everything in John's vision are symbolic (vs 12–14). These earthquakes and 'heavenquakes' signify the shaking and collapse of a 'home' built on godless attitudes and ambitions. When does it happen? All the time, at the personal and individual level and, at the end of time, at the cosmic level.

Thus the picture of people frantically seeking somewhere to hide (vs 15–17) signifies not a terrible destroyer-Christ, but rather that moment of disclosure and reckoning when all the lies, mockery and self-delusion about Christ, which are essential oxygen for atheistic secularism, are dealt with by 'the wrath of the Lamb' (v 16, a stunning paradox). This is the necessary judgement which those who 'suppress the truth' (Rom 1:18) draw down upon themselves. The distortion of truth is so grotesque that Babylon and the beast are made to seem more credible and desirable than heaven and Christ. Choices must be made. Jesus contrasts one kind of person – 'everyone who does evil [and hates the light] for fear that his deeds may be exposed' – with those who live 'by the truth [and come] into the light, so that it may be seen plainly that what he has done has been done through God' (John 3:19–21). To most of us this choice is a familiar cliché. Yet how easy it is to nod approval, but remain radically unaltered because undecided. George Macdonald warned, 'Nothing is so deadening to the divine as an habitual dealing with the outside of holy things!'[1]

WHO CAN STAND?

Revelation 7

Before proceeding to the seventh seal (8:1–5), John responds to the anguished question at the end of the sixth seal, 'Who can stand?' (6:17).

Taken together, the six seals conjure up an atmosphere of threat and anxiety. Everybody is damaged, either directly or indirectly, through the havoc created by the four horsemen as they ride the world. The fifth seal reveals a pilgrim church that must continue to traverse hostile terrain for a while longer. And, out of the sixth seal, godless self-deluding people are seen heading for a grim encounter with their creator. 'Who can stand?'

The situation takes another turn in as the four horsemen transform into 'the four winds' (7:1). Not winds from heaven, as we might expect, but winds 'of the earth' because, like their former manifestation in the horsemen, they originate out of, and are replenished by, the resources of human evil within the heart of the nations. They are surging, rebellious, demonic powers, straining to break loose on the world. We live among the four wind.: 'Who can stand?'

Four angelic guardians patrolling the edges of the earth hold the winds in check. How then do we encounter these winds? As a brooding menace; a chill shadow that can fall across our affairs at anytime; a mood of unease and indefinable apprehension; an idea at the back of my mind that it would not take much to tip my life over into chaos.

Certainly this ghostly feeling of a malign presence provokes anxieties and irrational gloom which are a familiar experience in our culture. Perhaps especially in a culture that has chosen to go it alone in the universe: self-creating, self-deciding, self-sufficient and most certainly self-glorifying. A closed, softly atheistic, windowless world of our own making in which life unwinds rather like the perforated programme roll in an old mechanical player-piano. The four evil winds are a real threat:

> Evil at its worst has a dynamic of its own which counter-feits the movement of praise. There is a logic of overflow in evil too, magnifying itself in a widening spiral and sucking up whatever it can into its destructiveness. Yet it is fundamentally inertial. It is parasitic and uncreative and on its way towards death it emasculates and paralyses. So, as William Styron says, writing of Auschwitz, it is an activity which leads to negation of all activity and life. Essentially, evil is not even interesting: it is a dull infi-nitely depressing vacuum which needs the skill of deceit to seem otherwise. Simone Weil wrote: imaginary evil is romantic and varied; real evil is gloomy, monotonous, bar-ren, boring. Imaginary good is boring; real good is always new, marvellous intoxicating.[1]

Certainly a dangerous aspect of the winds of human evil is their ability to practice 'the skill of deceit' and present evil in all its bogus attractiveness. 'Who can stand?'

The angels

When the four winds threaten to come storming out to tear up the earth, Christ's four mighty angels of providence hang on to them (Heb 1:14).

Angels. Our imaginations are not much helped by those images of curly-haired cherubs and limp adolescents draped with bed sheets, which pass for angels in the average churchyard. C S Lewis pictured an angel rather differently: 'a tornado of sheer monstrosities … darting pillars filled with eyes, lightning pulsa-tions of flame, talons and beaks, and billowy masses of what sug-gested snow, volleyed through cubes and heptagons into an infi-nite black void'. And in another description: 'pure, spiritual, intellectual love shot from their faces like barbed lightening. It was so unlike the love we experience that its expression could easily be mistaken for ferocity'.[2]

Such beings would be more than a match for the evil winds.

The angels of providence, protecting creation from the blight of human evil, in turn look towards the great angel of grace 'coming up from the east' (Rev 7:2), the symbol of resurrection. As the angel of the resurrection he marks God's faithful people with the seal of the Holy Spirit of resurrection (Rom 1:4; 8:11). It is the mark of Christ's overcoming, extended to all who follow him.

Here then at last is the answer to the question 'Who can stand?' All can stand who will stand by faith within the overcoming victory of our Lord Jesus, his cross and resurrection, 'through whom we have gained by faith into this grace in which we now stand' (Rom 5:2).

The great company

The sealing angel calls for space within the turbulence of the nations in order to place God's covenant mark of ownership and protection on his people. 'The Lord knows those who are his' (2 Tim 2:19): how else can we explain the astonishing vitality and growth of the church at times and in places of the greatest hostility? Why do people joyfully embrace Christ in the knowledge that their devotion to him will guarantee society's censure? At this moment across the world there are people turning to Christ and receiving in return the impress of the Holy Spirit of resurrection on their lives (Rev 7:3).

Yet clearly Christians face the onslaught of the crisis which is normative for the church in this world. This is the whole point of Revelation. In John's vision, the believers are 'they who have come out of the great tribulation' (v 14). Or, more precisely, 'who are coming through' (present participle). The testing is a prolonged process, and these Christians are described as having just stepped out of their trials and into glory, ie through martyrdom. The fires of testing are the price we pay for following Christ; the seal of the Holy Spirit guarantees that Christ will keep us not *from* the fire but *in* the fire: 'you will not be burned; the flames will not set you ablaze' (Isaiah 43:2).

The great company of Christ's overcoming people appear in symbols of purity and victory, wearing white and carrying palms (Rev 7:9). The victory is a spiritual one – the victory of their faith over every kind of threat and inducement to play it safe, abandon

Christ, and go with the flow. 'The great tribulation' is happening all the time. It is the conflict of loyalties in which our commitment to Christ can be made to appear fanatical, narrow-minded and doctrinaire, downright absurd or, in the severest test of all, an implied criticism on our unbelieving loved ones. The person who 'stands' amid all this confusion, who can keep hold of Christ as the revelation of God and the crucified Saviour, may be said to have 'washed their robes and made them white in the blood of the Lamb' (v 14).

They are therefore described in a symbolic number of perfection and beautiful symmetry, 12 x 12,000 (vs 4–8), like Israel drawn up on parade. A symbol which is in fact a countless reality, 'a great multitude that no-one can could count' (v 9). They are the people who made their choices while in the world and followed Christ, whatever the cost. Their first reward, having come through their great tribulation, is an astonished realisation, a gasp of delighted recognition, that the things they had believed in, prayed for, sung, practised, preached and witnessed to while they were in the world, are here. Faith gives way to sight.

How will *we* feel at that moment? Dante suggested that we will be like children in a kind of incredulous daze:

> The young are subject to a 'stupor' or astonishment of the
> mind which falls on them at the awareness of great and
> wonderful things. It produces two results – a sense of rev-
> erence and a desire to know more. A noble awe and a
> noble curiosity come to life.

For the great company of overcomers, their personal vision of Christ, which has accompanied them through their life of faith, unites with this cosmic vision in an interaction of praising and knowing (vs 12, 15–17).

Not that Christians are concerned merely to escape with their souls as they shelter in the bunker of the church. The opposite is the truth: to be sealed with the Holy Spirit roots the believer in Christ's incarnation and passion, which will engage us with the anguish and complexities of this world. We are sealed in order to serve.

We are now ready to proceed to the climax of the sequence of seal visions.

THE ARSONISTS

Revelation 8:1–5

The seventh seal is the final act in the present age, according to the 'seals' sequence. Christ breaks it open: we expect a cataclysmic event. In fact there is silence 'for about half an hour'! But it is by no means true that when God seems passive and silent that nothing is happening. The silence may be the judgement. God's 'active inaction' is at least as fearful as his loud interventions and big, storming judgements. For there are times when he takes his hands off people and their affairs, and 'gives them over' to the lifestyle they demand. Divine permission can be a terrible thing if it leaves us 'free' to pursue our imaginings and desires, with all the inevitable consequences (Rom 1:24). The consequences are not God's judgement in terms of distress, disease, conflict or unhappiness. The removal of his restraint, his silence, is the judgement; the rest is self-inflicted: 'Do not ... take your Holy Spirit from me' (Psalm 51:11).

But there is another side to this brief silence. Scene-shifting is taking place: seven angel trumpeters are moving into position ready to launch the next sevenfold vision sequence out of the final 'seal' event.

God calls for silence; he turns down the volume of the cosmic din in order to listen to the prayers of his people as they come up to him mingled with the angel's incense of worship. Suddenly our ideas of prayer as a serene, inner activity are blown away by heaven's astonishing response to the prayers. Dangerous and revolutionary powers are released at the throne. The angel-priest has scooped into the censer blazing coals from the great altar of incense, swung it around to fan the fire and tossed the flaming contents back onto the heads of God's enemies on the earth. The praying people are protected by the seal on their foreheads (Rev 7:3).

The conflagration and panic are described in classic, apocalyptic pyrotechnics: 'peals of thunder, rumblings, flashes of lightning and an earthquake' (8:5).

Here is a dazzling picture of what goes on when Christians besiege heaven in prayer. They move from the insignificant and irrelevant margins of affairs into their centre. Prayer puts the believer in touch with the deepest mysteries of world processes and events. Praying Christians are the real aggressors, setting the earth ablaze with the dangerous fires of God's purposes in the power of the Holy Spirit.

We tend to regard prayer as a sort of spiritual fire brigade, whose purpose is to dampen down the bushfires caused by godless powers. In fact the truth is quite the reverse. The real arsonist is the man, woman or congregation who brings specific situations, mingled with the incense of worship, to the throne, asking in Christ's name for the will of God to be done. It is the tyrants and megalomaniacs who struggle to douse the fires of God's purposes.

When he tried to hold together the lovely, slow-incense character of prayer, with its violent fires, George Herbert uses no less than twenty-seven images in his haunting, startling, serenely gentle, ecstatic, rich meditation on prayer:[1]

> Prayer the Church's banquet, Angels' age,
>   God's breath in man returning to his birth,
>   The soul in paraphrase, heart in pilgrimage,
> The Christian plummet sounding heav'n and earth:
>
> Engine against th' Almighty, sinners' tower,
>   Reversed thunder, Christ-side-piercing spear,
>   The six-days world-transposing in an hour,
> A kind of tune, which all things hear and fear:
>
> Softness, and peace, and joy, and love, and bliss,
>   Exalted Manna, gladness of the best,
>   Heaven in ordinary, man well dressed,
> The milky way, the bird of Paradise.
>
>   Church-bells beyond the stars heard, the soul's blood,
>   The land of spices; something understood.

How can we learn potent, revolutionary, fire-of-God praying? The answer is in the incense. Christ is himself the incense, 'a fragrant offering' (Eph 5:2), just as Christ is the priest who offers the incense and who 'brings fire on the earth' (Luke 12:49). He prays ceaselessly and perfectly for the world and for the church. He prays as each of us ought to but never do (Heb 7:25). And not only does he pray for us, but he prays within us, standing among us as one of us. He is our Saviour, saving us in every aspect of our existence, not least in our prayer life. He will not leave us at the mercy of our confusion over prayer.

Christ adds his prayer life to ours; he opens up his praying to take in ours to mingle with his, indeed to become his. Thus he is continually covering and converting our poor inadequate prayers. He offers our prayers with his own to the Father. Our voice mingles with his as we 'pray through the mouth of Christ' (John Calvin). Our prayers are unscrambled, cleansed, directed, redeemed by his, and raised to a far higher power in his.

Our prayers can have this fire-raising power when we participate in Christ's intercessions. At this moment the sensitive Christian will be directed as to *what* to pray for (Rom 8:26–27), as we allow the Holy Spirit to communicate to us 'the mind of Christ' (1 Cor 2:10–16), tuning our desires and thoughts to his. This mysterious, wonderful spiritual process is indicated in our familiar conclusion to prayer, 'We ask these things in Jesus' name'.

The fire spreads

The seven seals sequence is one description of God's activity in the world as he moves all things towards their destiny. It concludes with Christians engaged in potent and revolutionary prayer, causing fire to come from heaven. This scene triggers the next sevenfold vision and another way of interpreting events as the vehicle of God's purposes.

THE TRUMPETS

Revelation 8:6–12

Jesus Christ is not prepared to be the world's doormat, and his gospel is not a football that society can kick into touch with impunity. This much was made clear by the seventh seal which revealed Christ on the offensive, pouring fire onto the earth.

In his person, in his words, works and signs, culminating in his cross and resurrection, Jesus Christ confronts men and women with a crisis of decision; it must be yes or no. He is not merely available to society like a spiritual lubricant to keep the wheels turning.

> Love and the glory of God do not have the task of helping the world go its own way. The aim of Christians freedom is not that society should be better or function better. This may well come about ... but Christian freedom is not established in order to help people find an illusory replica of freedom to think that they are free outside Christ, and apart from him. This would be an abominable deception under cover of love, understanding and service. The good news of the kingdom is not a programme for reorganising the world but marching orders for every generation'.
>
> (Jacques Ellul)[1]

Hence the vision of the seven trumpets.

A trumpet blast is an urgent warning to wake up and get ready before the approaching crisis overwhelms us. The crisis was pictured in the final 'seal' event as God's blazing coals falling to the earth. The first three trumpet blasts develop this theme of Christ on the attack. They share a common motif of fire falling from heaven, producing effects on the world like the Egyptian plagues (Exod 7 – 11). The descending fire is drawn from Ezekiel's vision of blazing coals tossed over the rebellious and doomed city

(Ezek 10:2, 8). Both these Old Testament events portray the consequences of stubborn refusal to repent in the face of God's patient loving kindness.

The first trumpet (Rev 8:7) signals fire falling upon the earth which is smitten by the Egyptian plague of lightning mixed with hail. Limited damage occurs ('one third'). The second trumpet (v 8) announces a blazing mountain crashing into the sea which turns to blood. The third (v 10) has the effect of making freshwater bitter and undrinkable; and, on the fourth trumpet (v 12), the Egyptian plague of darkness is repeated. What do these things mean, for John's churches and for ourselves?

There are two interpretations at least, and both have powerful significance for the way we read God's hand in events.

1 The trumpets, naturally
We can take the trumpet events as a series of natural disasters that touch the land, the sea, freshwater and the sky. In each case damage is limited ('a third'), showing that these disasters are not God's final word of judgement, but shock tactics to shake people out of their earth-dream that life in this world is everything. This is a severe interpretation of natural catastrophe, that God allows destructive events in creation as an irritant to our comfortable world-bound view. John's world had Vesuvius; we have the Kobe earthquake. Both are permitted as megaphone calls to come to our senses and get our lives onto permanent foundations.

Earlier (6:10) John called enemies of the church 'the inhabitants of the earth' who have made themselves completely at home in this world order. Again, we must stress that it is never the Christian's task to reinforce this delusion. Rather, we dare to believe that anything, however distressing at the time, which can bring people who are entranced by this present age out of their stupor is nothing less than an act of the greatest love.

Jesus, himself, was clear about this: let no one imagine that he had come to bring peace. No, he brought a sword: division in families, fire on the earth and the cosmic baptism of suffering. He also advised that we learn to fear nobody except 'the One who can destroy both soul and body in hell' (Matt 10:28, 34–36; Luke 12:49–50). No one touched the nerve of healthy fear more than Jesus. His words are a trumpet blast. No one can turn his back on Christ and expect to carry on with life as before. God in his love will act. He will send the fire of crisis mixed in with some of nature's scary moments.

Yet what are we to make of the human cost (Rev 8:8–11)? Can we believe that the God of infinite love allows loss of life as an object lesson to those who survive? On this point, New Testament attitudes differ vastly from those of our own culture. Caird writes: 'The idea that life on earth is so infinitely precious that the death which robs us of it must be the ultimate tragedy is precisely the idolatry that John is trying here to combat'.

Each one of us will die. However long or brief our time, and by whatever means we meet our end in this world, by martyrdom or in a quiet nursing home, death places the same question mark against each of our lives (20:11–15). What is written about us in the heavenly books? What judgement will God give on our lives at his great throne?. Everything in our culture (medical care, insurance policies, retirement schemes, etc) conspire to keep these ultimate questions about eternity out of our minds. Surely then, it is a great mercy that God 'should send men from time to time forceful reminders of the insecurity of their tenure' (Caird).[2]

2 The trumpets, reflexively

A second way of reading the four plagues is to see them as metaphors for disillusionment, as 'inhabitants of the earth'.

Looking at the four plagues and their effects, the word which comes to mind is 'spoiled'. Earth, sea, rivers, sky – the entire circle of life is touched and spoiled, contaminated. Everything in life is disturbed and thrown into confusion by the demands of the gospel and the consequences of man's refusal to believe. The gospel is the spoiler because it introduces eternity into life's equation.

The principle idea is 'Wormwood' (8:10–11) which renders drinking water bitter and poisonous. If Christ is rejected, what is left is not merely his absence but a positive quality of bitterness that infects everything for the individual. As such, it is a reflexive, self-imposed judgement. If Christ's presence brings sweet-as-honey communion with the Father, his absence will eventually create a sense of disappointment and frustration, a real taste of bitterness. It can only be so since, in Augustine's words, 'Lord you have made us for yourself and our hearts are restless until they find their rest in you'.

Here, in other words, is the sword, and fire, and alienation predicted by Christ. If not immediately, the disillusionment is ticking away like a bomb waiting to explode. In Isaiah's striking image:

> ...as when a hungry man dreams that he is eating,
>   but he awakens, and his hunger remains;
> as when a thirsty man dreams that he is drinking,
>   but he awakens faint, with his thirst unquenched.
>
> (Isaiah 29:8)

'We had fed the heart on fantasies, the heart's grown brutal from the fare' (W B Yeats). This is our common experience as men and women who are created in the image of God but who resent his interference. We spoil the lives we believe we are saving when we keep them from God. It is our common experience, and usually mixed with a certain wistful sadness and nostalgic sense of loss. Again, Yeats conveys the bitterness powerfully:[3]

> ...Now my ladder's gone,
> I must lie down where all the ladders start,
> In the foul rag-and-bone shop of the heart.

On this interpretation, the first four plagues, when seen as haunting metaphors of self-inflicted distress, need not happen. Indeed, John uses powerful and disturbing imagery so that we might be jolted awake and out of our deadly self-delusion while there is still time.

These two interpretations of the trumpets belong together, occurring side by side throughout the present age. The message is carried to us as natural catastrophe threatening our physical well-being, and as images of a tragic sense of spoiling.

HYBRIDS FROM HELL

Revelation 9

At this point the screech of an eagle commands our renewed concentration (8:13). It is saying, 'Be ready for something even more hair-raising than the first four plagues. Prepare to see how God allows evil to be evil's own destruction.' John uses extreme imagery to expose extreme conditions. What follows is less like a day out in Disneyland than a visit to your nearest gallery of modern art.

The fifth trumpet announces venomous insects which swarm out of the Abyss (9:1–3). The message is 'Look at what people do to each other when they are in revolt against God'.

The Abyss

We first encountered the Abyss as the sea in Old Testament symbolism, an immense sump at the heart of the human race (see p 39). Caird vividly explains the Abyss as 'the infernal reservoir fed from the springs of human vice. It is the collective bad conscience of the race ... it represents the cumulative power and virulence of evil, to which all people contribute and by which all people, whether they choose or not, are affected ... from it come the haunting and avenging furies'.[1]

This is a very unflattering analysis of our fundamental problems as human beings. How much more pleasing if we could move the centre of trouble away from ourselves onto, say, defective resources: defects in education, government, housing, employment, and so on. But John's Abyss will not allow it. Defects are, of course, significant, but they are secondary. At heart, our disorders are not due to defects (which could be overcome by improved conditions,) but to *defection*; not defective resources, but our own revolt against God's mastery which shatters the fundamental life-giving relationship of human existence.

John's justification for such a radical diagnosis is grounded in Christ's teaching. Jesus located the source of evil not 'out there' among fallen spiritual beings, and not even in Satan, but 'in here' within the human heart (Mark 7:20–23). It is we who contaminate our spiritual environment, and not the other way around.

What is true of us as individuals is merely multiplied when it permeates the texture of our corporate life in our political, social and economic institutions. They too are susceptible to godlessness and a kind of demonic possession whenever they embrace ambitions and practices which are a slap in the face of the Creator. It is this negative, hostile, corrupt spiritual 'dimension' of some of our organised activities which Paul calls 'the principalities and powers', and which John describes as 'a fallen star' (Rev 9:1). Thus the mind and spirit of corporate life in revolt against God's government becomes the agent allowed by God to unlock the Abyss. That is to say God permits men and women to act out their schemes, even godless ones, yet persuades the outcome to further his own plans.

Venomous, demonic, familiar

Clouds of locusts swarm from the Abyss. They are no ordinary locusts, as in the Egyptian plagues or Joel's vision of the locusts of judgement. These locusts attack people, not crops. They have a venomous sting like a scorpion; they are demonic insects (vs 3, 5, 10). The Abyss has emptied its contents onto the earth's surface. This is our 'woe' – hell reaches above ground. Yet the most startling feature of these hybrids from hell is their faces – *they look like us* (v 7).

Evil can take countless manifestations but finally we trace it back to ourselves. We sting, and we are stung, for evil has a way of attacking and destroying its own perpetrators with demonic venom. The only protection from these swarming human-locust-scorpions is under the seal of the Holy Spirit of Christ's Overcoming (7:2–3; 9:4).

The description reads like a script for a Spielberg horror film, yet who of us would seriously question its validity as a diagnosis of the events of our own recent times? The poisonous insects with the human faces swarmed dramatically at Auschwitz and Treblinka, again in Stalin's arctic gulags and during the crazed genocide perpetrated by the Khmer Rouge in Cambodia and, more recently, in the programmes of ethnic cleansing in Bosnia and the carnage of tribal conflicts in Rwanda. But also in a million less spectacular instances of our everyday cruelty towards one another, like scorpions who sting and are stung.

Pascal – mystified (as we all are) at the Jekyll-and-Hyde, part-angel, part-demon contradiction within our nature – referred to humankind as 'the glory and the scum of the universe'. The shocking thing about this description is that few people today are seriously shocked by it. George Steiner asks us to ponder the enigma of an ordinary man, a loving family man, who picks flowers for his wife in the meadows, enjoys listening to Bach and Mozart and reading good books, and yet can go off each morning to put in a hard day's work killing hundreds of men, women and children in the gas ovens of Ravensbruck.[2] What are we to make of this? A scorpion with a human face is as near as we can get.

> Pessimist! Cosmic annihilation again? Not at all. I am
> afraid of 'hands fighting for the people which the people
> themselves will cut off'.
>
> (Czeslaw Milosz)[3]

No, not cosmic annihilation, but the effects of our perverse behaviour towards one another, though thankfully limited by God ('five months', 9:10).

So we could go on and on, piling up examples in support of John's grotesque but profound portrayal of us as venomous creatures. At the close of this century, optimistic humanism is utterly discredited as a serious analysis of our human nature; it is hopelessly naive and simply untrue of events in recent times. These events have worked a deep streak of disillusionment and cynicism into our culture.

That fifth trumpet blast is saying something like this: 'Look around you, and within yourself. Obviously there is something wrong with the way we are. Not merely defective, or flawed, or imperfect; but there is in us a perverse bias towards what is harmful; and energies are at work within and among us which can fairly be called demonic. We are like scorpions with human faces. Cosmetic alterations won't do. We must turn, repent with the whole of our being and seek a metamorphosis into real human beings, by abandoning our idolatries and exalting God as our God'.

The deep resources of darkness

And still John has not finished. The sixth trumpet (v 13) calls our attention to another alarming fact, mysterious and yet self-evident. It is the resilience and tenacity of evil which is able to draw upon immense resources.

His analogy this time is with the current historical, political and military situation. John takes up the fear in his world of attack from the formidable Parthian armies in the East 'at the great river Euphrates' (v 14). The East was to Rome what, say, Russia was to Hitler or Babylon to ancient Israel. The threatened populations were neurotic about the imagined countless hoards massing to attack them at any moment (vs 15–19).

But now John is talking about an army from hell, symbolised as four angels tethered at the Euphrates awaiting their moment of release when they can fall upon their victims in the West (vs 13–16). This enemy, evil, will not be worn down through the steady drip-drip of good. Creation awaits its redemption (Rom 8:18–23) through a final and decisive conflict that will flush out the last vestiges of evil and destroy them at the battle with Gog and Magog (Rev 20:7–9).

Yes, but what does this mean for us in our daily lives? Who or what are the four angels? What, where are these satanic resources of evil?

The answer in each case is to be found in the mystery of human idolatry, and the way we dethrone God and give his rightful worship to created things (9:20). This is so commonplace to us that we do not easily see what is implied. Things which become, in Jesus' words, our 'treasure', and 'where your treasure is, there your heart will be also' (Matt 6:21). It releases an ominous spiritual chemistry: idolatry bestows an illicit status and value upon mere created things, thus making them a focus and outlet for demonic activity that leads inevitably to spiritual and moral disorders (Rev 9:20–21).

The conclusion is this: the satanic resources, 'the four angels at the Euphrates', are as wide and as entrenched as human idolatry. This is why evil seems to be so resilient and ingenious, always disappearing but never completely going away. It seems to be defeated in one place only to reappear wearing a different mask, in another. But of course, as we have been saying, evil is not an 'it' which exists 'out there' somewhere but the product of an idolatrous human heart.

Thus the sixth trumpet is calling upon us to open our eyes to the facts and the reality of virulent evil. To acknowledge our personal participation in stockpiling the resources of evil by our own sinful idolatry, and to repent and enthrone God in our lives.

Yet we must reject despair as vigorously as we reject utopianism. The fact is God is in control. The damage and the poison is confined (vs 5, 15, 18). The gospel invites everyone with enough sense to come in out of the rain, to seek a deep and radical healing from the poisons coming out of the Abyss.

Jesus said, 'I have given you authority to trample on snakes and scorpions' (Luke 10:17–22).

THE SMALL SCROLL

Revelation 10

When the trumpets fail to stir an impenitent people (9:20) God turns to his secret weapon. More megatons of apocalyptic doom-laden warnings?

In fact these were on his global agenda – as the cycle of seven thunders announced by the great angel, heard and understood by John – but suddenly cancelled. John was on the point of fixing their irreversibility by writing them down when the order came, 'No! Delete it!' (vs 1–4). God will spend no more time on yet another layer of stern divine discipline extending throughout the span of the present age along with the seals, trumpets and bowls. He will not prolong the distress of the present age any longer: 'If the Lord had not cut short those days, no-one would survive' (Mark 13:20). Humanity, it seems, is content to trundle along unrepentant, endlessly spawning the means of its own unhappiness and destruction. But now John is told to break up this grim, inevitable flow of the consequences of our revolt, because this is exactly what God himself has done. Jesus burst in and mastered the old immutable law of sin and death (Rom 8:1–8).

No more delay (Rev 10:6)! Watch now how God brings forward the incredible and revolutionary way of the gospel of grace.

The secret weapon

The 'little scroll' clearly concerns the entire created cosmos, because the angel stands straddling land and sea (vs 2, 5), and he invokes God the Creator of all heaven and earth (v 6). Evidently the small scroll has universal significance.

John takes the scroll, and his next action tells all – he eats it (v 9; see Ezek 2:9 – 3:3). He takes it into himself, it nourishes him. The small scroll *becomes* John; he experiences it, embodies

and incarnates it. And he does all this as a *typical* representative
of the church throughout the age. John eats the scroll, which
means each Christian eats it. Thus the small scroll is the great
scroll transposed into the 'flesh and blood' daily life of each
believer. If Christ's overcoming Lordship (the great scroll) is to
impact upon the people around us, it requires a body, a demonstration in daily living (the small scroll).

Therefore John finds the small scroll to be a sweet and sour
experience (Rev 10:9–10). It is both delightful (it has all the glories of the gospel) and yet stomach-turning (the cost of faithful
witness). Jesus witnessed to the truth and glorious wisdom of the
Father's way of redeeming the world: the world extracted the
highest price for his faithfulness. Our witness is as Christ's witness. Like yeast, salt and seed we are hidden in the world, bearing witness to Christ as the way, the truth and the life. It is not
only a commission for us to 'go', but a real, lived participation in
Christ's complete self-abandonment to the ways and wisdom of
the Father. They are ways which expose the false visions, the hal-
lucinations, which fire the rebellious human mind. Thus 'your
king comes to you, gentle and riding on a donkey' (Matt 21:5) –
a ludicrous way of setting out to conquer the world! He reigns
from the cross – an incredible enthronement!

Hence the bitter-sweetness of authentic witness. Not that there
is any innate merit in suffering. Neither John nor the rest of the
New Testament ever teaches that. But, only be true to Christ, and
you will find yourself on collision course with the hostile mind of
the world. The lived graces of love, compassion, generous forgiveness, joy in waiting on others, irrepressible delight in God,
and a positive resistance to corruption in any form – these will
witness powerfully against the self-glorifying spirit of our age.
Some people will see and be moved to join us. But we should not
expect too much in the way of admiration! Christ was born to be
'a sign that will be spoken against' (Luke 2:34). His true people
can expect similar treatment.

The seals, trumpets and, later, the bowls are really an extension
of Old Testament prophetic ministry which railed against sin and
brought the sky crashing in on the unrepentant. But God's
favoured way is to set his gospel people in the midst of humanity,

to be as Christ: 'When they hurled their insults at him, he did not retaliate; when he suffered he made no threats' (1 Peter 2:23). And so Paul could describe his own experience as God's witness: 'When we are cursed, we bless; when we are persecuted, we endure it; when we are slandered, we answer kindly' (1 Cor 4:12–13).This is to eat the little scroll. *We* are God's secret weapon. *We* are the living sign of the King and his reign. *We* are 'the mystery of God [which] will be accomplished' (Rev 10:7). *We* are the most improbable means of bringing down God's enemies. *We*, the church, are the anvil which wears out all the hammers used on it.

This is the message, demonstrated and proclaimed for 'peoples, nations, languages and kings' (v 11).

The small scroll – the crucified mind

To consume the little scroll is a way of saying that we will do the Lord's work in the Lord's way. A way, said Paul, which seems foolish, ineffectual and lacking in all cleverness and sophistication. Most of all, it is a way of strength-in-weakness (1 Cor 1:18–25). It is the way of the servant, not the conqueror.

The Japanese theologian, Kosuke Koyama, makes a scathing attack upon the failure of Western mission in Asia to come with the crucified mind of Christ and the wise-foolishness, powerful-weakness of the cross. We are, he says, stuck in the crusading mind-set:[1]

Evangelism has not made any significant headway in Asia for the last four hundred years because Christians crusaded against Asians. When did Christianity become a cheap military campaign? Who made it so? I submit that a good hundred million American dollars, a hundred years of crusading, will not make Asia Christian.

What is this crucified mind?

It is the mind of Jesus Christ. It is not a persecution complex. It is not a neurotic mind. It is not a stingy and condemning mind. It is not a paternalistic mind. It is a two-way-traffic mind. It is a mind of self-denial. It is a community-building mind. It is a mind saying, 'In dying I come to you.' It is a mind obedient to the command, 'Go therefore.' If we have this mind, people will see it. People are perceptive. They will ask the secret of this crucified mind. This is evangelism.

Our Christianity has become a one-way-traffic religion. Jesus Christ is not a one-way-traffic Lord. It is not people out there who need repentance. It is, first of all, we who need repentance. We are far more arrogant than the people on the street. We are bigoted. We are prestige minded. We are money minded. We want to be called 'doctor', 'bishop', 'president'. We are self-righteous. We want to teach. But we do not want to learn. Christianity suffers from a 'teacher complex'. We are uglier than we think. We are becoming more and more blind because we say we can see (John 9:41).

To 'eat the little scroll' means:

- I will go with Christ, wherever he leads.
- I will go as Christ, whatever the cost.
- I will think with the crucified mind of Christ, however self-emptying.

THE WITNESSES

Revelation 11

God will demonstrate his own truth to the world through Christ's witnessing people. For, as Newbiggin said, 'the only hermeneutic [interpretation] of the Gospel is a congregation of men and women who believe it and live it'.[1] Or, as we have learned to say, people who eat the small scroll.

The temple in Jerusalem was in ruins by this time, destroyed by the Romans; but John still uses its imagery to describe a 'protected vulnerability' for Christians in the world. He 'measures' the inner area of the temple, and the altar, and the worshippers (v 1). 'Measured' signifies protected. God protects our inner life from spiritual harm.

But the outer precincts and the rest of the Holy City are left 'unmeasured' (v 2), unprotected, signifying that the church is open to whatever physical, economic or social attack she may be required to suffer as a price for her faithful witness. We know John is talking of persecution because he uses his usual code number (from Daniel) for the duration of a time of oppression – '42 months ... 1,260 days ... three and a half days' (vs 2–3, 11; see pp 7–9).

Severely oppressed, but the church is free with her inner 'measured' freedom to prophesy (v 3). In those circumstances 'prophesy' means to take up the cross and walk Christ's way, to mirror to a hostile world the power and wisdom of the cross which seems to the natural mind pathetic weakness, an irrelevant foolishness (1 Cor 1:18–25).

The two witnesses

Not every Christian will be called upon to die for their faith. John pictures two witnesses, a proportion of the entire community of believers. They are like olive trees whose oil, their love for Christ, feeds their own lamps (Rev 11:4; Zech 4:14). Light streams from them, and although at the mercy of their enemies, the two witnesses are endowed with remarkable spiritual powers. Their words are potent, scathing, challenging, unmasking, like fire,burning off the delusions of godlessness (Rev 11:5). The effect is comparable to Elijah and Moses (v 6) whose plagues aimed to bring their society to a change of heart. In fact the two witnesses are the aggressors in their clash with their persecutors (8:1–5). They scare the wits out of the dark powers when they stand in the market-place and 'implore you on Christ's behalf: Be reconciled to God' (2 Cor 5:19–21). The most extraordinary comment on their influence in society is that 'these two prophets had tormented those who live on earth' (Rev 11:10). The fire and sword of prophetic witness give society no rest.

The blood of the martyrs

The way of the cross and the life of the crucified mind bring a strange sort of 'success'. They are the way of faithfulness in living and speaking for Jesus. They are not a technique that can guarantee church growth or improve a Christian's standard of living.

> Let us never forget that in its first and mightiest conflict against the powers of this world, represented in the imperial might of Rome, the victory of the Gospel was won not by the cleverness of its preachers and theologians, and certainly not by its programmes of social justice but by the blood of the martyrs … [also] in the USSR … in China … in Latin America where the blood of countless martyrs has been shed in witness to the Gospel against cruel and unjust dictatorships.
>
> (Leslie Newbiggin)[2]

Growth and 'success' there most certainly are, but achieved in ways the wise of this world will never understand – through the 'weakness and folly' of the cross, and by participation in Christ's resurrection. This is the paradox of the authentic church.

> For to be sure, [Christ] was crucified in weakness, yet he
> lives by God's power. Likewise, we are weak in him, yet
> by God's power we will live with him to serve you.
>
> (2 Corinthians 13:4)

It seems that the church is in the world to be as Christ was: to provoke the powers of antichrist, to draw their (the powers') spiteful attacks, and thereby to expose them in turn to the power of God for their destruction.

Secret powers

Imagine the thoughts of an ordinary Christian before a Roman judge. At that moment it might occur to him that perhaps Rome is the best bet after all, and the gospel of love is simply a charming fantasy, no match for Roman might.

Therefore John unmasks Roman imperial power, so that every Christian might understand its true nature. Rome is 'the beast that comes up from the Abyss' (Rev 11:7). This is the beast's mode, always, in relation to human organisation. The creature is continuously in the process of emerging from the Abyss. In each generation it is easing itself into the world as it infiltrates available human systems. We have encountered the Abyss (the pit, the sea) before (9:1–3): it is the reservoir and resource of evil that constantly supplies human wickedness. Secret powers operate behind human facades.

Later, in chapters 13 and 17, John will have more to say about the beast. For now, we recall that the four monsters of Daniel's vision (Dan 7:15–28) were the four empires of the ancient world which had, in turn, conquered the Holy City of Jerusalem.

> [The] biblical history of the monster, then, begins in the
> original Babylon and ends in the latter day Babylon,
> which is Rome. For wherever men lay claim to despotic
> power; refusing to acknowledge that they are responsible
> to God for the use to which they put it, there the monster
> rises from the Abyss.
>
> (Caird)

By this reckoning, the beast is alive and well and at work in our world. It is a possibility waiting to be realised in any political system inclined to delusions of grandeur. The monster awaits the right conditions of godless arrogance which will allow it to incarnate itself in that system, movement or corporate life. Perhaps we should each write to our Member of Parliament suggesting that he or she ponder the possibility of a creature from the Abyss in our time!

The great city

In John's mind, Rome was demonised by its misuse of absolute power and its killing of Christ and his witnesses. Their bodies are symbolically left on display in the streets of 'the great city' (Rev 11:8). This city, like the creature from the pit, exists wherever human activity is organised and driven by motives which are in blatant defiance of God's laws or which apathetically disregard them. 'The great city' is a succession of times and places throughout history – Sodom, Egypt, Babylon and, for John, Rome. It is the spirit of the tower of Babel which, elsewhere, John describes as 'everything in the world – the cravings of sinful man, the lust of his eyes and the boasting of what he has and does – comes not from the Father but from the world' (John 2:15–17). It is a Christ-crucifying place. Just as his executioners celebrated Christ's death, so also the people who control the 'city of this world' throw parties for one another in mutual congratulation for ridding society of the nuisance of those prophesying witnesses (Rev 11:8–10). But we should remember that there is more than one way to silence troublesome prophets: remove them from the public square; restrict their influence in education, politics and, most certainly, in the media.

The witnesses follow their Lord into rejection and martyrdom; and they follow him into the real life of eternity. For their enemies, there are only the familiar repercussions of judgement (vs 11–13), designed to awaken people to the truth while there is still time. God allows evil to be evil's own destruction: that is the thrust of this passage about Christ's two witnesses (vs 1–13). By absorbing the spite of God's enemies 'in the streets of the great city', they become catalysts for their enemies' downfall. Reflect for a moment on the truth of this principle as we have seen it in the anti-God systems of our time. The church thrives while her old ideological tormentors wither away.

The seventh trumpet

At the final trumpet of the series we are in heaven amid ecstatic celebrations that 'The kingdom of the world has become the kingdom of our Lord and of his Christ' (v 15). Here we view current events from alongside the throne. God's people adore him for what they see. Their doxology mingles the divine qualities with the hard realities of our world where the nations 'were angry' (vs 16–18). But on earth the old problems persist. How can Christians announce that their God reigns when evil is so manifestly rampant? If we are saying that Jesus is Lord over the church and in heaven, but he is not Lord over the nations, then he is only a figurehead who does not actually rule.

Christ is truly Lord over everything in all creation, outside the church as well as inside. His victory over all the powers that disrupt creation was total and complete at his incarnation, but at present this is concealed, a 'veiled manifestation'. Christ revealed his kingdom by his words, deeds and signs – yet not in an incontrovertible way so as to leave people no choice but to assent whether they like it or not. The key to this mystery lies in the fact that the kingdom is not spatial or static, but a dynamic concept – God's rule in action. It is inextricably bound up with Christ's own person. The kingdom invaded society in his presence and ministry. Because Jesus was in their midst, the kingdom was in their midst (Luke 17:21); because he was near, the kingdom was near (Mark 1:14–15). The kingdom of God 'has both come and is still to come because Jesus has come and is to come again' (Cranfield).[3]

The kingdom – eternity spliced into the present

It is, therefore, more true and helpful to understand the reign of God not as moving from little to much, from partial to complete, but from veiled to manifest, from hidden to revealed, from unknown to known, from something denied to something acknowledged. The kingdom in all its fullness came in Christ because Christ came fully. We do not pray for something more complete to come, but for what is already complete to be revealed in all its power and glory – for the King who is among us incognito to stand forth in his majestic splendour.

'Your kingdom come': our hope does not move from less to more. The kingdom does not follow the process of development, evolution or progress. It is there already, but out of sight. This truth has tremendous implications for evangelism and mission. Our part is to witness, to tell and show the reality of Christ's Lordship by participating in his saving and healing works (eg Matt 10:5–8). We are not trying to bring in the kingdom or speed up its final disclosure by our programmes or crusades. It is here, awaiting disclosure.

The difference between the church and the world is that Christians are those to whom, by the sheer mercy and grace of God, the kingdom is being revealed, while the world consists of those who have not yet had their eyes opened to see it. From one moment to the next God may snatch aside the curtain for us to see the kingdom which was 'there' all the time.

Returning to the doxology in John's vision (Rev 11:15–19), here is the truth about the King and his reign, as seen from the other side of the curtain dividing time from eternity. What they see so clearly in dazzling light, we believe from scripture and bear witness to by faith.

A doxology in Siberia

Before he died in a Siberian camp in the 1940s, Archpriest Gregory Petrov wrote his 'Akathist of Thanksgiving', an ecstatic hymn 'Giving glory to God for everything!' Everything? Even the miseries of a Siberian labour camp?[4]

O Lord, how good it is to be your guest:
It is good in your home on earth, joyous to be your
    guest...

Glory to you for the feast-day of life,
Glory to you for the scent of lilies-of-the-valley and roses,
Glory to you for the sweet variety of berries and fruits,

Glory to you for the diamond sparkles of morning dew,
Glory to you for the smile of light awakening,
Glory to you for life unending, herald of heaven...

Life's tempests hold no dread
For him in whose heart shines the lamp of your fire.
All around, foul weather and gloom,
Horror and wailing of wind,
But in his soul, serenity and light.
Christ is there! And the heart sings: Alleluia.

Glory to you, who have shattered the power of the spirit of
    darkness,
Condemning all evil of destruction.
Glory to you for your revelations,
For the fortune of feeling your presence and living with
    you...

That is essential Revelation. Like Caesar, Nero and other despots, the KGB discovered that though Christ's true witnesses seem such easy targets in their 'unmeasured' life, they are invincible in their 'measured' inner lives. Christ's people see the truth, and the truth sets them free. This vision of the truth renders their tormentors powerless to harm them. Even when they are standing in that terrible Siberian cold, Christ's people know that 'Sovereignty over the world has passed to our Lord and his Christ, and he shall reign forever!' (Rev 11:15). It is a glorious vision which floods back in power and light into this present darkness, and we are released by it to live courageously for God.

Christ is there! And the heart sings: Alleluia.

WAR IN HEAVEN

Revelation 12

From the victory celebrations in heaven we cut away to a scene that contains the essence of spiritual warfare on earth. It has all the appearance of a hopelessly unequal contest: a pregnant woman against a murderous dragon.

Nothing could be more defenceless than this mother and her newborn child. She is the messianic community, and her labour pains are the dangers and sufferings endured by the true Israel as they await the advent of their kingly Redeemer (Gal 4:24, 27). She is the church in touch with 'the powers of the coming age' (Heb 6:5), powers by which she grows younger and younger with the life of eternity (Eph 5:25–32). At the end of this age she will be presented to Christ flawless and lovely. (In the second century 'vision' of Hermas, the church is pictured as an ancient woman – she possesses the wisdom of the ages – who, in complexion and form, is growing younger. She is eternally young, yet older than the world.)

Against the woman, and poised to pounce on the Christ child, is the dragon, 'the serpent, the devil, Satan' (Rev 12:9). He is God's ancient enemy and the disrupter of creation, the great deceiver, all voracious greed, heads, horns, claws and teeth. The dragon is described in terms characteristic of its earthly representatives: they are political-military powers. Thus the dragon's seven heads are numbered after Daniel's four monsters – three ones and a four. Its ten horns are those of Daniel's fourth beast (Dan 7:1–8, where Daniel's creatures symbolise the four great empires of his world). Jeremiah similarly sketched Nebuchadnezzar as a serpent which had swallowed Jerusalem and spat out the debris (Jer 51:34).

Diabolical panic

The Satan-dragon must, above all things, snuff out the threat to his domination posed by the woman's Christ child. As God continuously creates the cosmos, Satan strives to destroy it. As God creates all things good and beautiful, the devil distorts and perverts them. God plants a field of wheat, and the devil strews it with weeds. Above all else, Satan desires to deface the image of God in humankind.

Imagine then the demonic rage when there appears in the midst of the human race an individual who perfectly bears the divine image in his truly human nature, who does so on behalf of humanity and as their saving representative. Hence the chaotic panic in the fallen spiritual world of the principalities and powers (Eph 2:1–3) when that child, now a man, threatens to awaken the bewitched human family from its deathly sleep under the satanic influence (Eph 5:8–20). No wonder the dragon 'stood in front of the woman who was about to give birth, so that he might devour her child the moment it was born' (Rev 12:4).

Satan storms at the messianic community and her child. The awesome flare-up of demonic activity provoked by the presence of Christ as he went about his work is witness to the fact of God's invasion of satanic territory (eg Mark 1:21 – 2:12). This child has come to 'rule all the nations with an iron sceptre' (Rev 12:5).

So, while the contest between the satanic dragon and the child seems so utterly one-sided, 'our struggle is not against flesh and blood, but against the rulers, against the authorities, against the powers of this dark world and against the spiritual forces of evil in the heavenly realms' (Eph 6:12). And there is a power that will overcome the great enemy, but it is so extraordinary that Satan himself utterly misunderstood it.

To the hate-ridden demonic mind, Christ had surely fallen completely under his enemies' power when they nailed him to the cross. Now, it seems, the dragon devours the child-Redeemer. Crucifixion not only killed its victim but utterly humiliated and discredited him: it was a manner of the execution designed to obliterate every shred of dignity and reputation. The victim's cause was thus demolished along with him. Crucifixion allowed the caprice and sadism of the executioners full rein. On the cross, the full force of satanic spite slammed into Christ's defenceless body.

The cross attracted universal horror, disgust and ridicule in the ancient world. 'The enemies of Christianity always referred to the disgracefulness of the death of Jesus with great emphasis and malicious pleasure,' Hengel writes. 'A god, or son of a god, dying on the cross!' This incredulity is illustrated by a well-known piece of third-century graffiti depicting a young Christian, Alexamenos, who stands before a caricature of a crucified figure with an ass's head; the caption reads 'Alexamenos worships his god'. By the cross, Satan hoped to annihilate Christ and his cause.

'War in heaven' – the dragon hooked

Job coined the image of the leviathan (the dragon) caught on a hook (Job 41:1–2). In the fourth century it inspired Gregory of Nyssa's angling metaphor in which Christ is the bait on the hook of the cross. The cross totally outwitted Satan. It has a wisdom and power incomprehensible to the fallen spiritual powers: 'None of the rulers of this age understood it, for if they had, they would not have crucified the Lord of Glory' (1 Cor 2:8). So an event that happened in AD33 at a place outside Jerusalem is described by John in terms of its impact on the spiritual realm: 'And there was war in heaven'(Rev 12:7). The chaos-dragon, Job's leviathan, in its countless incarnations from Babylon to Rome and down to our times, is defeated and ruined by the crucifixion of Jesus Christ (vs 7–9). It is a moment precisely marked with the hymn, beginning '*Now* have come the salvation and the power and the kingdom of our God' (vs 10–11). Christians believe that world history hinges on Christ's victory over Satan on the cross.

And yet evil still thrives. Was it a real victory, or was it, as the critics of Christianity suggest, the church's fantasy? No. A fundamental and decisive change in the power structures of creation did take place in the cross and resurrection. But God has allowed Satan to exist as a fatally damaged being, doomed, running out of time and all the more dangerous because of it.

Fear of time passing

The effect of the cross on Satan is to provoke him to behave like a fatally wounded reptile which, in its frenzy and panic, becomes even more terrifying, lashing out in all directions in its death throes: the dragon is 'filled with fury, because he know that his time is short' (v 12).

Time is Satan's dilemma: time running out, his life running out. Ejected from the eternity of God's presence (v 8), he is unable to exist in any place (or person) where Christ dwells; he is ever driven out from those places where people live under the sign of Christ (v 11; 7:2–3). Satan is trapped in time and, in his fear, he rages against time passing away (12:12).

So the dragon lashes out at the messianic community, the New Covenant people who are, even now, in eternity, 'seated in the heavenly realms in Christ Jesus'. For our great enemy, the message that Jesus Christ, crucified and risen, has thrown wide the doors of eternity for all who will enter, is a maddening provocation.

Fear of time passing – illusions

If the manager of a store knows that certain crooked practices are about to be discovered and that he will certainly lose his job as a result, his anxiety will effect the atmosphere around him. Time is ticking away; he stands to lose everything; and the people around him will feel it. The spirit of the present age is like that. 'Sin occurs through man's self-willed greed for the world, and through his acceptance of the world which the devil conjures up as the ultimate ground and object of existence' (Schlier).[1]

In fact the illusion which Satan is able to project is a double distortion. We find ourselves making too much or too little of the world. Satan portrays world reality either as eternal delight or eternal death, everything or nothing. He induces either idolatrous reverence for the present or exaggerated despair and suicidal gloom. Creation is either the Alpha and the Omega for modern man, or, in cynical disappointment, he treats it with utter contempt. Either way, time is a problem: either it is rushing us through life to old age much too quickly, or it is boringly static. In the satanic illusion, falsehood and deceit permeate the seductive, distorted vision of life in the world.

> All those large dreams by which men long live well,
> Are magic-lanterned on the smoke of hell.
> William Empson[2]

The Satan-dragon is going down and is determined to take as much and as many as possible with him. The woman – the church – is the special focus of his hate: he 'spewed water like a river' (v 15) in an attempt to drown her. The water of the Abyss is his natural medium and it symbolises the torrent of lies and anti-Christ propaganda, the malicious gossip put in circulation to discredit Christ and his people. We can expect no less in our own time since, having failed to sweep the woman into oblivion, the dragon storms off 'to make war against the rest of her offspring' (v 17) including ourselves. But Christ keeps his people safe. Although he transcends the reach of the powers of this world (the child is 'snatched up to God and to his throne', v 5), Christians are already secure 'in Christ' and as safe now as they will be in eternity.

John compares our present relationship with Christ to the woman flying like an eagle 'to the place prepared for her in the desert' (v 14). We will have more to say about the desert experience later in chapter 17. For now we can note that the desert is the vantage point, the place of critical height above the present turmoil, from where believers can see the great city and the serpent for what they truly are. The demonic torrent of destructive lies has merely soaked into the sand (v 16), negated by Christian minds shaped and inspired by God's revelation: 'those who obey God's commandments and hold to the testimony of Jesus' (v 17). This is the stance of the 'church in the desert' and the subject of the following chapter.

ABYSMAL POWERS

Revelation 13:1–10

The ominous remark that 'the dragon stood on the shore of the sea' (v 1) calls our attention to the way Satan attacks the church throughout the present age. This sea is the dragon's natural environment, the cosmic Abyss of evil (11:7). Schlier strikingly calls it 'the sea of the world into which Satan looks and in which, recognising himself, he creates his own reflection'.[1] It is also the spawning ground of demonic reinforcements which the dragon now calls up. They appear in the form of two beasts, Satan's agents, the antichrists of John's world. By looking at their traits we will be helped to identify the manifestations of antichrist in our own time, for antichrist is always now, he is always our contemporary (1 John 2:18; 4:2–3).

The antichrist

The first beast called into action by Satan emerges from that same sea, the Abyss, on whose shore the dragon stands (Rev 13:1). This sea also signifies the western sea, the Mediterranean, the route by which the Roman Proconsul 'came out of the sea' from Rome and landed at Ephesus. Rome is, for John's world, the great abysmal power, satanically created and satanically endowed with enormous strength and authority.

Reading John's description, we see that the antichrist is a parody of Christ and his kingdom, matching him point for point and compelling us to choose between them. Christ came to reveal the Father and to do his will; the Rome-beast too is a physical manifestation of its invisible satanic master. Christ's resurrection is mimicked by the beast's recovery from near extinction (v 3) when Nero's suicide in AD68 plunged the Roman Empire into dangerous turmoil for a year. Christ is adored by his people; the beast is also a cause of wonder to the masses (v 4). Christians thank the Father for the gift of his Son; the beast's grateful followers 'worshipped the dragon because he had given authority to the beast' (v 4). Christians celebrate the saving power of the risen Christ poured out into the world by the Holy Spirit; the Rome-beast extends its reach and power into the nations with the athleticism of the leopard, the strength of the bear and the great tearing mouth of the lion (v 2). Satan's puppet agent is a cunning, brutish, voracious world power dominated by bestial instincts. It is the inhuman form of a degenerate political system, possessed and manipulated by Satan.

Another parody of Christ in the details of what the beast does in the world. Christ is the Word of God who speaks the words of life. The beast too is a mighty speaker, but his great speech is essentially blasphemous (vs 1, 5–8). Not only in the misuse of the divine names, and holy things, in profane oaths, but also in the blasphemy of misdirecting glory and honour away from God and onto the beast. This is what demonises a human activity or organisation.

The Roman emperor Domitian would begin a formal document, 'Our Lord and God orders this to be done', and titled himself 'Dominus et Deus' – Lord and God. This was a blasphemous and satanic distortion of the proper power and authority given to the state and its leaders by God as a means of protecting society from itself.

As we weigh these characteristics of the antichrist, we look around to see if they are incarnated in any of the powerful systems and phenomena of our world. John's picture of the beast, through which the dragon attacks the present, provides a further piece of evidence. Typically the beast makes 'war against the saints' (v 7). We can expect this activity at any time, 'for there is,' comments Schlier, 'a kind of metaphysical hereditary enmity between them (the Saints) and the beast. For the beast has taken over his hostility from Satan, its Lord'. State power, when penetrated and manipulated by Satan, is not only invariably anti-Christian and anti-gospel but usually seems to triumph. Its victory over the saints is assured (v 7) in the same way that its victory over Jesus Christ was certain by means of the political, religious and cultural systems of his day.

A third expression of satanic activity through the agents of the antichrist in society is in the drive to enfold the entire world within its domination. Christians today may have forgotten the missionary nature of their gospel, but the antichrist works to fulfil global 'satanic outreach' (vs 7–8). Where, in this century, have we seen this tendency in the world? Christ's claim that 'All authority in heaven and on earth has been given to me' (Matt 28:18) is counterbalanced by the satanic arrogance – 'All inhabitants of the earth will worship the beast' (v 8) to whom the dragon has given power and authority.

Choices

John goes on to acknowledge that when the kingdom of Christ is set against the kingdom of Satan, and life in the body of Christ is compared to life in the degenerate bestial body of Satan's domain, people may well choose the beast over Christ. The marks of the beast in blasphemy, persecution and the abuse and exploitation of power are no great problem for the nations. John compels the Christian to see that, for the mass of people, the benefits of subjection to satanic authority, exercised through the antichrist, appear to be considerable and carry none of the penalties and sacrifices attached to loyalty to Christ. But they are had only at an enormous price – in a word, 'freedom', of which the nations endlessly talk and naively dream. Outside Christ's reign, they will never know true freedom.

This was the issue at our Lord's testing in the wilderness: he was offered the world at the price of his soul (Luke 4:6). Give glory to Satan and everything will be yours. Christ exposed the offer as a very poor bargain indeed, and paid for his choice with his life. The irony is that the Rome-beast, the antichrist, which offers such benefits to its adoring masses, is itself shackled, and draws its life and strength from the dragon, its creator and·lord. The questions 'What is real freedom? Who is truly free?' are therefore fundamental in Christian witness when, as now, the great search is on for the holy grail of 'personal freedom'.

Decisions

John leaves his Christian readers in no doubt concerning the reality of the antichrist, its activities and its fate. He now encourages us to 'patient endurance and faithfulness' in the knowledge that the satanic captors will go into captivity and the satanic killers will themselves be killed (Rev 13:9–10). Christians will be able to discern the beast. We must not close our eyes to this disturbing teaching or plead ignorance of the beast's existence. We will not be surprised at the continuous undercurrent of anti-Christian sentiment in our culture, or when this breaks surface in more brutal expression. We will stand firm and patient in Christ in the face of satanic rage, knowing that this is no earthly conflict. As Satan destroyed himself when he tried to destroy Jesus Christ, so Christ's people are in the world to take that same prophetic stance, unmasking the antichrists, naming names, interpreting the dragon's panic as his time runs out.

Who are our antichrists?

The traits of the antichrists of John's era reappear in the great totalitarian regimes of the political Left and Right, which have devastated the nations in our own time. Less obvious are the claims, implicit in our modern omnicompetent state, which come close at times to the spirit of the antichrist. Listen to the messianic tone of the politicians around election time! What they offer is virtually a parody of Christ's kingdom with their promises of a happy life from the cradle to the grave, without the slightest reference to God as a serious player in their schemes.

Even less obviously, the authentic spirit of antichrist infests the pervading secularism of our society. It is very difficult to pin this spirit down, or to say precisely what it is, but not at all difficult to see its effect everywhere. If antichrist strives to negate the people of God, then secularism as a mind-set, as a world view, fulfils the role of antichrist in a society where we seldom suffer physical punishment for our faith. Thomas Howard writes: 'the "secularisation" of life, urged on us by science and commerce and modernity generally, is surely one of the bleakest myths ever to settle down over men's imaginations', and he goes on to point out that our battle with antichrist is waged over the meaning of ordinary, everyday life. To overcome the deadening spirit of antichrist that drives secularism, 'we will have to recover the sense of the hallowed as being all around us. We will have to open our eyes and try to see once more the commonplace as both cloaking and revealing the holy to us. We will have to refuse resolutely the secularism that has made ordinaries unholy. We live in a dark age, and somewhere in this world there have got to be lights burning in shrines and on altars, bearing witness to the presence of the holy'.[2]

PR FOR THE ANTICHRIST

Revelation 13:11–18

The antichrist requires a public relations company to push its cause on the mainland where John's churches live. Enter the second beast 'coming out of the earth', 'the earth signifying the indigenous provincial administration (v 11). Thus the demonic network of influence now stretches from the dragon, through the beast from the sea (Rome), to the beast from the land (local government) and so into homes, schools and the market-place.

The second beast looks harmless enough, a 'lamb' with no menace or power to frighten. But its function in the satanic scheme of things is to complement the beast from the sea. It adds its two horns to the ten horns of the first beast (v 1), thus perfecting its power. And the lamb speaks 'like a dragon' (v 11). So much for appearances! The second creature is spokesperson for its master, the first beast. Its special task is to spin words, translations, explanations to justify the ways of the first beast to a bemused populace. It sounds like the dragon in the local dialect.

Do not be taken in by appearances. Dangerous powers can be packaged under attractive logos, such as a cuddly lamb. Close your eyes to the images and attend carefully to the words. What spiritual strategies are being smuggled in under the flow of plausible speech?

Because of its promotional and propagandist role, John later refers to the second beast as a 'false prophet' (16:13; 19:20; 20:10). Jesus warned of chaos when 'false Christs and false prophets will appear and perform signs and miracles to deceive the elect – if that were possible' (Mark 13:22).

A political priesthood

Thus a political system can make itself available to corrupt spiritual powers, and its political activities take on a real spiritual dimension. John may be using bizarre symbolism, but these are symbols of concrete realities. The second beast, the 'false prophet', functions like a political 'priest', mediating between the dragon and the populace on the mainland. Power needs a validating ritual to give it a divine sheen: 'the blending of the ritual institution with the administrative was a leading idea of the practical organisation of the Imperial period' (Schlier).

To work this magic the political system, which is the second beast, apparently had access to remarkable spiritual powers by which to perform 'great and miraculous signs' (Rev 13:12–14). Neither Jesus nor John contradict this claim. In his exhaustive study on the work and gifts of the Holy Spirit, James D G Dunn writes: 'There is no lack of claims to phenomena outside early Christianity which parallel the Pauline charismata in varying degrees of closeness ... there was nothing distinctively Christian in charismatic phenomena themselves'.[1] It is *love* that is the distinctively Christian mark.

The image makers

The false prophets of the political system have successfully projected a compelling image of the first beast: such signs and wonders, such resilience in surviving its near-death experience (v 12, see p 82). The people are persuaded that their best interests lie with the beast from the sea. They 'set up an image in honour of the [first] beast' (v 14).

Look carefully at how John speaks about this image. In fact there are two images, two representations of Rome. The first is the ritual image of Caesar and his power, which a devotee would find in a temple dedicated to the imperial cult. The Roman emperor, who insisted on being worshipped as God, would be honoured with a pinch of incense in the flame of his shrine. People obliged him, but probably went on with their household gods anyway.

The second image, which arises out of the first, is far more significant: the false prophet 'was given power to give breath to the image of the first beast, so that it could speak' (v 15). The image comes alive and acts in a parody of God incarnate in Christ, within the minds, imaginations, value systems of the population. This living image 'has intelligence and produces intelligence; it appeals to the feelings, the reason and the will of its worshippers. It not only intoxicates the masses but also provides scholars with new and unforeseen tasks, it inspires the poets and it arouses speculations … the image speaks words of admonition and consolation' (Schlier).[2]

The conjuring trick is complete. The bestial empire formed in the image of its lord, the dragon, is by the false prophet's 'honeyed song and reasoned argument' made to appear worthy of trust and worship. Its domination of physical and spiritual life seems total, even to the extent of deciding who lives and prospers and who does not (v 15). The state now has a way of distinguishing its friends from its enemies and has ritual justification for punishing those (Christians and others) who refuse to toe the line.

But the beast cannot be entirely sure of its worshippers.

The mark of the beast

John sees society paying a tremendously high price for the benefits of living under the beast. The creature places its indelible mark '666' across everything under its sway (vs 16–18). John clearly expects his readers to have no trouble in deciphering this number, although it 'calls for wisdom'. We are not so fortunate, and the experts have expended incredible ingenuity on determining its meaning!

'To mark' was a technical term used for the imperial stamp on commercial documents and for the impress of the emperor's head on coins. Another intriguing solution suggests John was calculating the numerical value of the inscription on the coinage of Emperor Domitian. Perhaps the most satisfying explanation is that when the Greek name for Nero – Neron Kaisar – is transliterated into Hebrew characters and these are given their numerical equivalents, they add up to 666.

The mark was placed on the right hand or forehead (v 16). The right hand signifies trade, buying and selling, and work. Without the mark on the hand, it is not possible to earn a living. Slaves were branded on the forehead, but as a sign of disgrace, not loyalty. In the fifth century BC, prisoners of war were known to have been branded on their foreheads by their captors. There is also the suggestion that John had in mind the high priests of the imperial cult: a priest 'wore the imperial image on the golden circlet on his brow and on his signet ring' (Stauffer). Taken together, these colourful references suggest that loyalty to the beast was required of everyone. The beast wants every single person, without exception. A person's life depended upon that mark.

It goes without saying that John is not suggesting a literal physical mark on the skin visible to the eye. He is, as ever, using rich imagery to convey concrete reality. The mark of the beast is a travesty of the seal of the living God placed upon his people (7:2–3), and there lies our clue to the real mark of the beast. Just as God's seal of the Holy Spirit is evidenced in love, joy, peace and faith, so also the mark of the beast is a pattern of attitudes, perceptions, hopes and value systems, cut into human behaviour in line with the ideas put about by the false prophets.

'666' in practice

The big, bad examples of the mark of the beast in society are well-known in the tyrants, totalitarian regimes, serial killers, and so on, of our own recent times. Yet for most of us, in our ordinary daily lives in a democratic society, the influence of 'the false prophets' of '666' is likely to be a much more low-key process, more deadening than overtly deadly, but effective nonetheless.

The spirit of false prophecy can, of course, inspire 'other gospels' and thus try to play havoc with our faith. But, like all subtle advertising, and because the nature of false prophecy is deception and lies (13:14), this spirit is able also to create spiritual confusion by means other than blatant head-on confrontation. It is the master of the 'honeyed song and reasoned argument' which is at least as subverting to faith as strident atheism. False prophecy can brand the mark of the beast on human behaviour by covert persuasion, surreptitiously soaking our imaginations with suggestions that tap into deep-rooted drives and aspirations. Certainly the technology is in place for it.

Perhaps a trivial, even banal, example can make the point better than a solemn, philosophical one. Consider the omnipresence of consumerism with its environment of media-driven images. A well-known television commercial for a certain soft drink involves a charming group of children of different nationalities, each holding a can of the drink and singing, 'I am the future of the world; I am the hope of every nation'. The child or the drink? A Christian journalist asks, 'Why does no-one cry blasphemy? Is it because we are blind to what has happened to us? Is it because our much-vaunted sophistication and ironic detachment is incapable of protecting us from the seduction of images, the idolatry of consumerism?'

Consumerism which appears gentle as a lamb, but which speaks with the voice of the dragon and effectively brands forehead and right hand with its mark. In particular, consumerism requires a constant stream of a 'socially stimulated desire for novelty and excitement ... the effect of the media is not to elicit belief but to maintain the apparatus of addiction to the commodities that alleviate boredom' (Christopher Lasch).[3]

'666' gradually...

John has described a process by which the beast comes to power in a society and imposes its mark upon it: false prophecy, image, the image coming to life, domination. Christians concerned for the well-being of society will stay alert for the first signs of a similar process emerging in their own time.

In his study of the Holocaust, Richard Neuhaus points to the gradual pace and patterns of events leading up to the catastrophe which, more than any other event, has passed into our folklore as the epitome of '666', the mark of the beast in a society:[4]

> The Holocaust was not the abstraction we call a period of history, but a succession of mornings and afternoons and evenings much like this day. It was a tangled combination of innumerable actions and consequences, of careers and ambitions, of fears and loyalties, of flirtations with the unthinkable turning into routines of the unexceptional. To most of those involved, the icon of evil did not present itself as whole. It happened an hour at a time, an equivocation at a time, a lie at a time, a decision at a time, a decision evaded at a time.

This calls for wisdom (v 18). And it calls for an answer, a divine rebuke to the creeping gloom spread by the predatory activities of the Satan-dragon and his mob.

'WHERE I PAY DEARLY'

Revelation 14:1–5

Crisis will be the usual condition for a church whose Lord was 'a sign that will be spoken against' (Luke 2:34). Crisis strips away what is unimportant: it is a make or break point where Christians will either overcome or compromise. It is the moment George Bernanos had in mind when he said, 'I believe only where I pay dearly.' At a time of crisis the church has the possibility of really being the church. For John's Christians crisis came in the form of the domineering '666'.

A Japanese Christian points out that in his script the character for 'crisis' is a combination of the character for 'danger' and 'opportunity' (or 'promise'). Crisis is therefore not the end of opportunity but, in reality, only its beginning – the point where danger and opportunity meet, where the future is in the balance and where events can go either way. But how many of us, when compelled to choose, would identify with the rejected Christ, and prove to ourselves the sincerity of our love for the Lord by 'paying dearly'? The answer is '144,000'. This figure is a hieroglyph, a beautiful and symmetrical number, indicating in fact 'a great multitude that no-one could count' (7:4–9). They are the Lord's faithful witnesses who take the conscious risk of putting their experience of the Father's name on public view (14:1). To say that they number '144,000' suggests their special quality and precious value.

> Here lies a piece of Christ; a star in the dust;
> A vein of gold; a China dish that must
> Be used in heaven, when God shall feast the just.
> (Robert Wild, epitaph for the grave of a godly man)

We have already noted that there is very much more to Christ's witnesses than mere dogged stoicism under pressure (see p 70). Living under the Father's name, they expose the various antichrists and Satan's battle plan. Such glowing tributes are easy for us to say, but if we are to emulate them we will need similar clarity of vision and gutsy, primitive New Testament simplicity in dealing with Satan and his hordes. 'Resist the devil and he will flee from you' (James 4:7; 1 Peter 5:8–9). Martin Luther, who had a wonderfully earthy theology in these things, advised:

> The best thing you can do is to tap the devil on the nose at the very start. Act like a man who, whenever his wife began to nag and snap at him, drew out his flute from under his belt and played merrily until she was exhausted and left him alone.

There is a tune we can play which drives off the beast: it is called the 'new song' (Rev 14:3).

'I shall be made thy music'

The new song has an ancient pedigree. In Isaiah the song celebrates (even while Israel was still in her Babylonian captivity) the Lord's liberating march through every form of human existence and on to the ends of the earth (Isaiah 42:10–17). It is a song woven of signs and wonders. As we would say today, Christ has visited every corner of creation to declare his victory over all our demons (Eph 4:9–10). Stale worship is an appalling discourtesy to God, but avoiding it is not a matter of forever churning out new hymn books or avant-garde worship styles. Good worship requires good worshippers; the new song requires new singers.

In fact the song is not new. It cannot be, because its theme was everlastingly decided when Jesus entered the conflict between God and Satan and won the decisive victory for the Father and his creation. As the grace of God breaks through to us in wonder upon wonder, like glimpses from a universe of love and light into this dark world, our song will be, yes, oven-fresh every time.

And yet perhaps we are a little uneasy at the prospect of all those massed choirs endlessly praising! After a while our tired imaginations jar at the thought of continual sameness. But heaven is life in the presence of God who is 'making everything new!' (Rev 21:5). There, worship will not be something we strive to do so much as something we become, or are in the process of becoming, with no discrepancy between what we have in mind and what we are able to do.

In this present life, God's loving desires towards us run into the obstacles of our darkness and suspicions and our sheer, dense, stupid inability to receive them. But in his new creation in heaven:

> God's work will there be like music in the hands of a master, the mere utterance of his mind. The redeemed will be that living music, through their perfect response to his will. Each one will know God through the entire obedience of his own heart to God, God who works all his works in him.
>
> (Austin Farrer)[1]

In this life we make music and sing our new songs as best we may. But the moment is coming when 'I shall be made thy music' (John Donne). In which case this present life of ours is, in reality, a time of learning, practice and rehearsal for the big performance in eternity:

> Since I am coming to that holy room,
> Where, with thy choir of saints for evermore,
> I shall be made thy music; as I come
> I tune the instrument here at the door,
> And what I must do then, think here before.[2]

Death, in this vision, is not the loss of all we have been gaining, but the winning of all we have been hoping.

Hoping for what exactly? Whatever the details, surely everyone longs for his or her life to add up to something: to realise the message encoded by creation and redemption within them; to fulfil their meaning. Yes, and these hopes will be realised in the transformation of the new creation when we step through the door of death and are 'made thy music'.

What does John Donne mean by 'I tune the instrument here at the door'? Austin Farrer suggests that we practice real praise now by the simple attitude of enjoyment:[3]

> The best way of thanking God is to taste his goodness
> with all our palate. It is no use making speeches of thanks

to a musician, if you are bored by his performance. You
may deceive him, indeed, if you are a clever hypocrite,
and can act the attention you can't be bothered to bestow.
But God reads our hearts, and he knows whether we taste
his kindness, or not. Enjoyment is the sincerest thanks.

This holds the secret of future praise, begun now and brought to
perfection when we have been 'redeemed from the earth' (14:3).

But can we really apply these words to ourselves when it
appears that John has in mind exclusively celibate males?

A holy war

Remember, John is writing a pastoral letter to churches under
attack, a Christian community fighting for oxygen within the
enveloping fog generated by the false prophets of the antichrist. It
is a tough calling and military metaphors are appropriate.

John's puzzling words (v 4) are, like most things in Revelation,
a symbol drawn out of the Old Testament, in this case from the
regulations for holy war laid down in Deuteronomy (chapter 20;
23:9–14). Israel's warriors were required to consecrate themselves for conflict through ceremonial purity. John takes up this
tradition as a symbol of moral and spiritual purity from the seductions of the antichrist he calls 'Babylon'. The celibacy he requires
of his people is sincerity of heart.

From the idea of the soldiers' ceremonial consecration for holy
war, John moves easily to the language of obedience and sacrifice
(Rev 14:4). In practice this meant 'no lie was found in their
mouths; they are blameless' (v 5). No compromise, no double-
thinking, no hypocrisy, no dividing up the interior life, no play-
acting, no private wish-world which cannot be translated into
prayer. Positively, it means that the springs of sincere desire that
drive our inner life are opened up and entirely surrendered to the
living God. Thus we fulfil our calling to be the Lord's witnesses,
for our lives will follow a similar trajectory to his life, moving to
resurrection by way of our cross.

ANGELS OF PERSUASION

Revelation 14:6–20

The vision swings back to the present and to the church with its strange, original stance in the world. These Christians definitely mean to win the Roman world for Christ. They refuse to be intimidated, and they will not be confined within imperial limits. The gospel exerts its tremendous logic on their minds and, in the metaphor of three messenger angels (vs 6–13), we are shown aspects of Christian presence in the world which many of us perhaps would rather not know about.

The angel of evangelism

An angel 'flying in mid-air' (v 6), halfway between heaven and earth, is a symbol of the church as a go-between messenger, proclaiming the 'eternal [unchanging] gospel' into the shifting sands of our human situation. Here is the whole church taking the whole gospel to the world. Not content simply to proclaim into empty space, but to proclaim so that people are left in no doubt about the seriousness of their response (v 7). This is the church under pressure from the message burning in its heart, the people of God bursting with news to tell.

> The heights of heaven cannot contain your presence, yet
> you have a dwelling in my mind. I try to conceal your glo-
> rious name in my heart but my desire for you grows till it
> bursts out of my mouth. Therefore I shall praise the name
> of the Lord as long as the breath of the living God is in
> my nostrils.
>
> (Solomon Ibn Gabriol)[1]

Angel of prophecy

The church in each generation is there to announce to 'Babylon' that 'Babylon is fallen (v 8) even while the Babylonian way of life seems very much alive. The fall of Babylon in Isaiah's time (which underlies John's use of 'Babylon' as a symbol of antichrist power) was the longed for signal of Israel's emancipation:

> Day after day, my lord, I stand on the watchtower;
>> every night I stay at my post.
> Look, here comes a man in a chariot
>> with a team of horses.
> And he gives back the answer:
>> Babylon has fallen, has fallen!
> All the images of its gods
>> lie shattered on the ground.
>> (Isaiah 21:8–9)

Only the fall of 'Babylon' can release those who are addicted to the 'maddening wine' (Rev 14:8) of her glitz and power and success. 'There is no hope for the rehabilitation of the alcoholic until the source of his supply is cut off' (Caird).

More exactly, because of Christ's conquest of the satanic powers, Babylon's former citizens may respond to the great gospel invitation to come and try the sparkling wine of the New Covenant:

> On this mountain the Lord Almighty will prepare
>> a feast of rich food for all peoples,
> a banquet of aged wine –
>> the best of meats and the finest of wines.
>> (Isaiah 25:6–8)

Come and take the Lord's cup of salvation. The early church believed that our Lord's miracle at Cana, when he turned the water into wine, is the key to the rest of his mission, his words and his works. Come and drink the Lord's wine of praise.

> I have invited you, Lord, to a wedding feast of song,
>> but the wine – the utterance of praise – at our feast has failed.

You are the guest who filled the jars with good wine,
    fill my mouth with your praise.

(Ephrem)[2]

The choice is therefore between the 'maddening wine' of god-lessness or the 'wine of praise' that Christ offers in the cup of his salvation. To declare that 'Babylon is fallen' is an invitation to escape Satan's grip, to come and enjoy the living God and magnify him with the praise of our lives.

Angel of consequences

What was the secret of the first Christians' missionary fire? A tremendous motivation for vital witness is given here in the picture of people who refuse the gospel invitation, but choose instead to stay enmeshed in the life and downfall of 'Babylon' (Rev 14:9–13).

At this point language fails in trying to express the indescribable, for 'If words fail in describing the possession of eternity, must they not also fail in describing the privation of it?' (Caird). The angel has no pleasure in saying what he must say, but sketches a shocking and repellent picture *in order to prevent it happening* (v 12). For the same reason John, throughout his Book, uses a range of grotesque and insulting images (dragon, beast, Jezebel, whore, etc) to shock the reader awake to the issues.

Whatever else Christians are for in the world, they are here to unmask the beast, depopulate Babylon and point as many as will take notice to heaven. The 'deeds' that accompany us to glory (v 13) will be our faithful testimony, our praying, weeping, loving, serving, befriending, helping, worshipping, proclaiming, reasoning, persuading, enduring.

What 'angelic' tasks will you undertake today?

The great winepress

The fact of a final reckoning – the judgement of our lives (vs 14–16) – touches the nerve of a thoroughly healthy fear. Jesus more than anyone else in the New Testament warned of the destruction to come upon selfishness.

But fear of death and of judgement to come will never of itself bring us the answer to our dilemma. Indeed, we may misunderstand entirely and, panic-stricken, rush about trying to live the perfect life. No, the clue is in the name of the great Harvester: of all his titles, 'son of man' v (14), means that Jesus is on our side, he is one of us. He is our man, our Redeemer-brother (the brother whose responsibility it is to redeem us, Heb 2:5–11), who always receives the lost and embraces the untouchable. We go to the judge to be saved from the judgement. It is the safest place to be.

Therefore though you slay me, I will trust in you.
For if you pursue my iniquity
I will flee from you to yourself
And I will shelter myself from your wrath in your shadow,
And to the skirts of your mercies I will lay hold
Until you have mercy on me
And I will not let you go till you bless me.

(Solomon Ibn Gabriol)[3]

It is the wisdom of fleeing to the one from whom we are in flight. Nevertheless, Christ poses the question to every generation: 'Will it be Caesar or the crucified Lord?' It matters how we decide and it matters for all eternity.

In terms of the harvest liturgy of ancient Israel, believers in any place are the 'first-fruit sheaf' taken out of the field of humanity (Rev 14:4, 15). The initial reaping was the signal for the rest of the harvest to begin (vs 14–16), ending at the Feast of Tabernacles with the grape harvest. The way John uses the symbolism, the grain harvest is blessed but the vintage is accursed (vs 17–20).

Christ's angelic forces drive the powers of the antichrist into the 'winepress'. God is depicted removing the restraints and allowing the self-destroying powers of evil to bring down what is not of him. John is a realist and what he pictures here is nothing more than realistic. He saw it in his time and we most certainly see it in ours. Antichrist is thrown into the winepress of God.

VIEW FROM THE FAR SIDE

Revelation 15

Another turn of the kaleidoscope and the drama takes the form of the Exodus. We are able to view proceedings from the best seats in the house, on the far side of the sea, among the great multitudes who went all the way with Christ (vs 2–4). Moses' exodus dramatises Christ's redemption. Here they sing 'the song of Moses [and] of the Lamb' (v 3).

This moment in the unfolding of the Revelation marks the beginning of the end of things. There is talk of one more series of seven actions, 'the seven last plagues – last, because with them God's wrath is completed' (v 1). But this time, because we can look back across the sea and interpret events in terms of the Exodus, the seven plagues (16:1) appear not as yet more doom and gloom, but as something 'great and marvellous' (15:1, 3), inspiring delight in saints and angels.

What Moses did for Israel in their dash for freedom from Egyptian slavery, Christ does for all who will trust and follow him. In John's vision, the pursuing Egyptian chariots are 'the beast and his image and the number of his name' (v 2) – a hostile spiritual culture that threatens to overwhelm the believing community and draw it back into bondage. Notice that our redemption is first, last and always an act of God, something he has *done*. All other aspects of authentic Christianity radiate from that once-and-for-all decisive act of redemption.

Exodus-redemption (the redemption in Christ of which Israel's exodus is the great picture) is not primarily an explanation of the meaning of life, or a philosophy, or a moral system, or even a therapeutic method. All such blessings are like the fall-out from the vast explosion which is Christ in his incarnation, crucifixion, resurrection and the poured out Holy Spirit.

In Christ, his faithful exodus-people are 'victorious over the beast'. They overcome by participating in the power and authority of Christ's decisive overcoming. 'God first gives what God commands,' Augustine said. He commands that we follow our Lord, surrounded by the marauding influences of 'the beast and his image and the number of his name', and in Christ he has given us the victory before we even set out on our faith journey (Rom 6:1–14).

The first question asked by the old Heidelberg Catechism[1] is 'What is your only comfort, in life and death?' Back comes the grand, plain response:

> That I belong – body and soul, in life and in death – not to
> myself but to my faithful Saviour, Jesus Christ, who at the
> cost of his own blood has fully paid for all my sins and
> has completely freed me from the dominion of the devil;
> that he protects me so well that without the will of my
> Father in heaven not a hair can fall from my head; indeed,
> that everything must fit his purpose for my salvation.
> Therefore, by his Holy spirit, he also assures me of eternal
> life and makes me wholeheartedly willing and ready from
> now on to live for him.

This is essential 'exodus' faith. Exodus-redemption runs like an organising, shaping, co-ordinating spine through the cosmic drama of the Revelation as well as through our own personal faith journey. Therefore even the dire 'seven last plagues' can be seen as playing their part in the exodus dynamic, in overcoming the influence of 'the beast and his image and the number of his name'.

Exodus – said and sung

The pursuing Egyptians brought about their own ruin when they reached out to recapture Israel. At the same stroke, the sea became the way of salvation for God's people *and* the means of destruction for their enemies. The sea parted for Israel and engulfed the Egyptian chariots (Exod 14). God can use the forces of evil to be the means of their own destruction. Thus by his death, Christ destroyed death; by his crucifixion at the hands of the 'principalities and authorities' he broke their power and 'led captivity captive' (Eph 4:8; Col 2:14–15). Hence Patrick Kavanagh's delightful image of Christ's resurrection as 'a laugh freed for ever and ever'. Laughter becomes our only possible response as we realise that, by his cross and resurrection, Christ has already and forever secured the redemption of all creation.

Therefore the sea is indeed a Red Sea 'mixed with fire' (Rev 15:2), the fire of God's decisive holy judgement on the hostile spiritual powers which, like Pharaoh's chariots, harass and hound Christ's journeying people. This truth, if we will allow it to break in upon our imagination, demands a song – an astonishing song (vs 3–4).

A consequence of countless believers following Christ through this world and into the next is that 'All nations will come, (v 4) in a worldwide turning to God. And if for 'King of the ages' (v 3) we take the strong variant reading 'King of the nations', it all points to a universal movement towards God which is tied up with the faithful witness of the church. A faithful church gives God his heart's desire that 'all nations' turn and seek him:

> Mission has its origin in the heart of God. God is a foun-
> tain of sending love. That is the deepest source of mission.
> It is impossible to penetrate deeper still; there is mission
> because God loves people.
>
> (David Bosch)[2]

Anyone concerned with the struggle for the soul of the world will want to think long and hard about these words in the exodus-song. We can tease out its meaning by asking how John imagined the nations would be drawn to God by the influence of the church. Is he suggesting that society will be bowled over by our high-powered mastery of electronic media in the service of evangelism? Or by our big battalions, hugely resourced? Clearly the answer each time is 'No'. John is describing something quite different.

For Christ – like Christ

Look again at the exodus-song. John calls it 'the song of the Lamb' – an extraordinary title when we think of the power, authority and majesty of exodus-redemption. The secret of authentic Christian power in the world is held in that image of 'the Lamb' – innocent, blameless, defenceless, suffering – which let loose unimaginable power by the cross and the empty tomb.

Satan had suggested other ways to Christ when he tempted him in the desert; his own disciples pleaded with him to pursue other methods to bring in the kingdom of God; the mass of people were agog for ever more sensational displays of power, of military and political might. But Jesus, the Lamb of God, went the way of the cross and released that laugh 'for ever and ever'.

When Christ's people 'walk as he walked' (1 John 2:6, RSV), they embrace Christ's way of power and transformation in the world. Then their innocent suffering will seem an odd, strange, ineffectual stance in a society driven by quite different notions of power and effectiveness. But God's 'righteous acts' (v 4) will be revealed through the day-to-day qualities of ordinary Christians, especially in the way they take evil out of circulation by absorbing it into themselves.

Christians are effective when they bear witness to a kingdom which is not of this world (in its motivations), yet which is able to suck the poisons out of the heart of this world. They know of a strength which, astonishingly, seems to come through weakness, like Christ who abandoned the outcome of his life to the redeeming ways of the Father (2 Cor 12:10). And this is the unusual quality and odd stance which, says John, will move the heart of the nations to turn to God. There is a tremendous and humbling challenge to our notions of power in this teaching (see pp 45, 46). Could it just be possible that we have got it wrong about Christian power, influence and impact in society?

Reflect for a moment on the difference between what we tend to admire as spiritual power today, and John's idea of the world turned to God by the witness of vulnerable, defenceless, outnumbered and outgunned Christians who mirror the way of Christ.

These thoughts take us back once more to that Exodus sea 'mixed with fire'. We said it was the fire of judgement on God's enemies, but it is also the fire of his peoples' faithful and costly witness.

> May the power of your love, Lord Christ, fiery and sweet,
> so absorb our hearts as to withdraw them from all that is
> under heaven. Grant that we may be ready to die for love
> of your love as you died for love of our love.
>
> (Francis of Assisi)

We are now at the beginning of the End. Still the heavenly temple
is inaccessible to us – sinful men and women who cannot endure
the immediate light of God's presence. 'And the temple was filled
with smoke from the glory of God and from his power, and no-
one could enter' (Rev 15:8). But the tempo is quickening, and we
are moving towards the consummation of history, the finale of the
cosmic drama of Revelation.

A CRASH OF IDOLS

Revelation 16:1-15

'Heaven for sparrows and Christians – the earth for us,' a triumphant Adolf Hitler announced. And God said to his angels, 'Go, pour' (v 1). Hitler's 'Babylon' went up in smoke.

The final series of 'seven bowls of God's wrath' focus on arrogant persecuting powers with delusions of godlike invincibility. They exist in various forms – political, economic, militaristic, ideological, even religious – thus the retribution of the seven bowls is neither about the judgement of individuals for their contribution to world guilt (which comes later, 20:11–12) nor about the collapse of the natural physical order. Instead it deals with the moment when God's patience with corrupt, idolatrous, impenitent systems finally runs out.

Notice the timing and the place of the seven bowls. Earlier we decided to interpret the seven seals and the seven trumpets as operating throughout the entire span of this present age. But the seven bowls are different. They were first briefly announced as imminent at the start of the Exodus passage (15:1 mentions the seven plagues, which are the contents of the seven bowls of wrath). Next, the exodus theme is developed (15:2–4), and only then does John return to the seven bowls of wrath in detail.

It suggests that the bowls correspond to the exodus crisis and the moment of irrevocable judgement when the sea engulfed the pursuing Egyptian chariots. The opportunity to break off their hostility towards Moses had passed, the talking was over, and the God-who-acts acted to deal with the impenitent powers we have learned to call 'Egypt', 'Babylon', 'the beast', 'Rome', 'the great city', 'the antichrist'.

Judgement is slow in coming, but in the event it is swift and decisive. The seven bowls move urgently towards their climax with only minimal details. The disturbing reality is that human systems can adore false idols to such an extent that they blur into these idols and become fatally demonised.

Won't leave, can't leave

John identifies the recipients of the poured-out bowls. In his experience they have several characteristics: they bear the indelible mark of the beast and worship his image (16:2); they kill God's witnesses (v 6; 11:1–12). They are full of stubborn blasphemy (16:9, 11, 21). There are societies which are so deeply enmeshed in the texture of their particular 'Babylon' that first they refuse to leave, and finally they find that they have lost the will to leave. They can only stay and share her fate.

Having said this, we need to be aware of the many times John speaks hopefully and optimistically about the repentance and conversion of people who in the past have been sworn enemies of God and his people (2:16, 21; 3:9; 11:13; 14:6; 15:3–4; 18:4). We recall his joyful song celebrating the expectation that 'All nations will come and worship before you'.

But on the impenitent New Babylonians four bowls of retribution are poured out. The contents of the bowls – their 'wrath of God' – are familiar to us by now: the means of sin become the means of sin's punishment, and sin is made (or allowed) to bend back onto itself and its perpetrators. Thus the branded mark of the beast breaks open into an infected 'ugly and painful sore' (16:2). And because idolatry and blasphemy are a fundamental disordering of reality, nature offers itself to God as an agent of his judgement. Bowls (vs 2–4) describe natural disorders; the sea becomes unusable (v 3); the fresh water becomes undrinkable (v 4); and the sun becomes unbearable (vs 8–9). Nature shares in God's outrage at stubborn idolatry.

Taken together, as symbols of the spiritual realities underlying Babylonian idolatry, these natural disorders are haunting images of the bitter disillusionment and anguish people feel at the collapse of their hopes.

Disillusionment? Yes and no

Patrick Kavanagh talks about 'God's delight in disillusionment', which sounds a horrible idea. Yet it is surely a great kindness if someone makes the effort to awaken us out of illusion, particularly if the illusion is a dangerous one. A rude awakening is to be preferred to a deadly dream. Rather, we should pray for God the Holy Spirit to come and disillusion us, our friends and our society before unreality becomes hopelessly confused with reality, and we, and they, are lost.

Jesus surely had this painful saving process in mind when he heaped congratulations on the heads of the poor in spirit, the mourners, the meek and those who hunger and thirst (Matt 5:3–6). These people had become aware, suddenly or gradually, that in fact they had nothing and knew nothing of eternal value. A shocking realisation of emptiness and need. Congratulations indeed to such people who have broken through the earth-dream, their illusions recognised and shattered, awake now to the God of truth who waits to receive them and bless them with the gift of the kingdom. God delights in that kind of redeeming disillusionment. It would be a devastating realisation that the pool I've been drinking from all those years (all those aims, values, motivations) is in fact nothing but a mirage – but it could be the beginning of wisdom (Isaiah 35:7).

There is a redeeming and positive disillusionment which says 'Yes' to life. But John is describing a different chemistry – a destructive, killing disillusionment which brings only bitter regret and anger. It is a 'No' to life – the death of hopes with no resurrection. Babylonian to the core, these people will stay and share in their Babylon's fate. Idolatry is a puff, a promise which never delivers.

Jesus again defined the principle at work here when he warned that people become what in their hearts they adore: 'For where your treasure is, there your heart will be also' (Matt 6:19–21). Be very careful what and where your treasure – that focus of your energies and hopes – lies, because your life is attached to it and will participate in its destiny. If your treasure is earthbound, it will crumble away into dust taking you – your essential self – with it.

If however you are a God-struck, God-centred person, you 'store up for yourselves treasures in heaven', and your true self will take on the same quality of everlastingness.

God delights in any disillusionment that will awaken us to that heavenward quality of life.

A tremor through the system

The sense of despair at being identified with the decline of the beast, so powerfully suggested by the first four bowls, now deepens. 'The throne of the beast' and the regime it symbolises come under attack.

Once before in John's lifetime the empire had experienced chaos and hysteria, 'plunged into darkness' (Rev 16:10) by Nero's suicide in AD68 and the power struggle that followed. The beast had survived that near fatal attack (13:3, 12), but the episode sent tremors through the entire system. People who trusted in the empire and the throne of the beast for the successful outcome of their lives now 'gnawed their tongues in agony and cursed God' because of the threat to their expectations. Underneath these images of political turmoil and physical pain there is a deeper spiritual anguish. As a Jewish writer said of the victims of the Egyptian plague of darkness, 'harder to bear than the darkness was the burden of their own selves'.

The pace quickens with the sixth bowl emptied 'on the great river Euphrates' (16:12), the eastern frontier from where Roman citizens feared the menacing Parthian armies would strike. More anguish for the beast's true believers.

John understood these political and military events, as Isaiah did in his time and place. Egypt and Assyria may have planned their campaigns and pursued their imperial ambitions, but Isaiah could see the hand of the Lord inside the glove of their schemes: 'the Lord will whistle for flies from the distant streams of Egypt and for bees from the land of Assyria'. The king of Assyria may follow his own thoughts but Isaiah sees him as an instrument in the Lord's hand, 'a razor hired from beyond the River [Euphrates]' (Isaiah 7:18–20). And now the Lord is at work again at the Euphrates, directing his angel to 'Go pour'.

The Lord has his hands immersed deep in the historical

processes. He is never remote from us, standing back from the rough and tumble of our world's affairs.

In the best possible light

Seven angels are at work pouring, out seven bowls of retribution on the beast and his network of relatives. The beast has his own slant on history and employs advertising agents, image makers, news managers and propaganda experts whose task it is to present events in the most favourable light for the beast (Rev 13:1–11; p 87*ff*). John pictures them as so many frogs, 'evil spirits of demons' (16:13–14) popping out of the mouths of the dragon, the beast and the false prophet (13:11–18). The frog propagandists use words and images that 'perform miraculous signs' (16:14). They are not the only ones.

> How interesting are you? How thoughtful? How heroic? Do you wish you were more interesting, caring, thoughtful, heroic than you are? If the answer is 'Yes' – and how could it not be – the Peugeot 406 advertisement is aimed at you ... the 406 is being sold not as a car but, like a pop single, as an emotion, or a series of emotions and aspirations – about being someone, somewhere, better than you are now.
>
> (*The Independent*)

Guard your mind.

The vision is urging us to attend to international events and to reflect on the astonishing crash of falling idols around the world at the present time. Behind the interminable news and media analysis, stay alert to other sounds of seals opening, trumpet blasts, a voice saying, 'Go, pour', and the sudden arrival of the Lord within events (v 15).

ARMAGEDDON

Revelation 16:16–21

Armageddon is the end of something if not the end of the world (v 16). There is life after Armageddon. Creation's story still has a long way to go before this physical cosmos is rolled up (20:6, 11). In popular imagination Armageddon is an emotion, a sense of dreadful destruction. It triggers apocalyptic images which are not far off John's description of events (vs 18–21): the Somme, Dresden in flames, Allied armour pouring across the night desert to destroy Iraqi forces. Is Armageddon still on God's agenda?

Armageddon – a place and a principle

There is no such place as Armageddon. The name means Mount Megiddo, which is puzzling because there is no mountain at Megiddo, a town some 30 km SE of the modern Israeli port of Haifa. Carmel is the nearest mountain. It seems that John is making a symbolic name by connecting Mount Carmel with Megiddo.

Ahab, a sort of antichrist figure and the husband of Jezebel (2:20), set the false prophets of Baal to battle against the God of Elijah at Carmel (1 Kings 18:16–40. The false prophets perished in the contest. Similarly, Josiah defied God and was slain at Megiddo (2 Chron 35:20–24). Taking these vivid associations together, we see Armageddon as a symbol of the endless struggle between truth and deceit. It stands for a place where lying, seductive prophecies and their practitioners go to meet their doom (Rev 16:14). It is first a principle, and then it is the outworking of that principle in an event or a succession of events. Wherever the word of God overthrows the entrenched spirit of antichrist, there is Armageddon.

John is describing a particular enactment of the Armageddon principle between the great political and military powers of his day.

Armageddon – what sort of battle?

John is convinced that, by her animosity towards Christ's people, Rome is unleashing into the world forces which will eventually bring about her own downfall. Like the prophets, he believed profoundly in the self-destroying dynamic of evil.

He is here concerned with the immediate threat to his churches. He writes his pastoral letter to assure them that the redeeming love of God is mightier than Roman eagles. At this level, therefore, John is not so much concerned with the end of the world but with the end of Rome's world. Caird writes about John's eschatological vision of the terrible seventh bowl released by the conflict of Armageddon:

> Broadly speaking, it is true to say that no prophet ever used eschatological language except to give theological depth and urgency to the historical crisis which he and his people are facing at the moment.

So, yes, John is anticipating a battle that will weaken Rome.

The sixth bowl had pictured a dried-up river Euphrates which becomes a highway for 'the kings from the East' and their armies (v 12). Perhaps John had open before him the significantly similar prophecy of Jeremiah concerning the end of Babylon:

> A drought on her waters!
> They will dry up.
> For it is a land of idols,
> idols that will go mad with terror.
> (Jeremiah 50:38)

This is precisely the predicted outcome of Armageddon when the Eastern powers struggle against Rome and her allies, 'the kings of the whole world ... on the great day of God Almighty' (Rev 16:14). The powers of idolatry lash out at Christ's people, but those idols 'will go mad with terror' at God's judgement. This is the Armageddon principle.

Talk of invasion from the east was in the air, along with a rumour that Nero had returned to life and was in Parthia plotting to return with a vast Parthian army to reclaim his throne (13:3).

John takes up this idea of the spirit of the depraved Nero infesting Rome's enemies with demonic ambitions for invasion and conquest. But, by the violence of the imagery that John is using to describe the consequences of the Armageddon conflict, we know he is signifying a spiritual disruption, a smashing of the spiritual principalities and powers. His apocalyptic language (16:17–21) indicates a time of cleansing when God sweeps away arrogant, godless, lying, idolatrous powers. Even then there will remain people who 'curse God' (v 21) because their hopes and security are so shaken by the challenge to Rome's authority. John gives us a sense of spiritual devastation.

Armageddon – when?

This is the question in the minds of every millennial doom-watcher. When will Armageddon happen? But we have stressed that it is a principle at work wherever idolatrous deceits confront the truth of God in human society. Whether at a cosmic or at a local level, Armageddon is the showdown when God confronts the lying agents of antichrist. In his perfect justice and loving commitment to the world, God knows when, where and how to draw the forces of darkness into the open for decisive conflict. And yet John does have important things to say about the timing of Armageddon.

Into his prophecy of invasion John injects a warning: 'Behold, I come like a thief! Blessed is he who stays awake' (v 15). Words which take us back to Jesus' warning to his disciples about the future destruction of Jerusalem: it will take everyone by surprise, so stay awake (Matt 24:43; Luke 12:39). The same urgency is required for Armageddon. The Lord is, of course, urging John's heavens to *spiritual* readiness (Rev 3:2, 18). It is not the Parthian invasion from the east that requires their concentration, but the possibility that they might fail to interpret the events as Christians should. It is not at all surprising that unbelievers would be thrown into panic and terror at the threat of invasion; but it is a scandal when Christians respond in this way. 'Stay awake!' Look, listen, interpret, discern the hand of God in the political processes. The Lord is coming within international upheavals. Do not go about like an idiot 'naked and shamefully exposed', but stay clothed and awake (16:15). Think with a Christian mind.

> The voice of the Lord strikes
>   with flashes of lightning...
> The Lord sits enthroned over the flood...
>   (Psalm 29:7, 10)

> Rise, Lord, judge thou the earth in might,
>   This wicked earth redress;
> For thou art he who shall by right
>   The nations all possess

> The nations all whom thou hast made
>   Shall come, and all shall frame
> To bow them low before thee, Lord,
>   And glorify thy name.

> For great thou art, and wonders great
>   By thy strong hand are done:
> Thou in thine everlasting seat
>   Remainest God alone.

>   (John Milton, 1608–74,
>   based on Psalms 82, 85 and 86)[1]

FATAL ATTRACTIONS

Revelation 17

A great shout goes up after Armageddon – 'It is done!' (Rev 16:17). Saints and angels dance on the ruins of Babylon.

John is concerned with Rome as one particular manifestation of that spirit of Babylon which runs through human affairs like a subterranean river, bursting out into the open at different times and places. These manifestations change continuously, but the spirit of Babylon is a constant which is first seen in biblical history inspiring the builders of the tower of Babel (Gen 11:1–9). Armageddon symbolised a decisive showdown between the forces of rebellious idolatry and the truth of God. Babylon's power over our lives, we are assured, is broken. Now the church can display an alternative way of living, inspired by the love of God. Like Christ's great victory cry from the cross, 'It is done!'

As we read Revelation, we are all the time striving to transpose the message from there and then to here and now, a discipline that raises several questions. Chiefly, if the shout 'It is done!' is to mean more than merely wishful triumphalism, we need to know more details. So John responds with chapters 17 and 18 in which he gives further explanation of Babylon's downfall.

Enchantments

More even than Rome's brute strength, John feared her powers of attraction. The imperial system was awe-inspiring (13:1–4). To make the point and to shock his readers awake to the dangers, he compared Rome-Babylon to an exotic seductive prostitute (17:1–2). Seduction is not something that we easily notice happening to us, which is why it is seduction! A Roman legion you could see coming, but who can detect a fascinating possibility stealing into one's mind?

> We are not free to choose by what we shall be enchanted,
> truly or falsely. In the case of false enchantment, all we
> can do is take immediate flight before the spell really
> takes hold.
>
> (W H Auden)[1]

But John is not convinced that Babylon's enchantments can be
detected and rejected that easily. And what if a Christian secretly
wants to be seduced by the dazzling woman?

> When we are falsely enchanted, we desire either to pos-
> sess the enchanting being or to be possessed by it.'
>
> (Auden)

Jesus experienced the full force of those spellbinding enchantments at the beginning of his public ministry, as if to signal that
his duel with Satan, the master of false enchantment, is the
essence of all our temptations (Luke 4:1–13). Jesus looked into
their mysterious depths and emerged qualified to diagnose the
kind of spell a person is under. There are bonds against which
mere reason can do nothing, especially where there is covert
acquiescence in being spellbound. Jesus came to 'proclaim freedom for the prisoners' (Luke 4:18).

While it is true that recognising idols for what they are does
not break their powers of enchantment, it can be the first step
towards our deliverance. The second step will be to go, like John,
'in the Spirit into a desert' (Rev 17:3).

The desert experience

Even John could only think straight about the dazzling woman,
Rome, when he was far enough away from her in a desert place
(v 3). From that critical distance he could see what was going on.
He was able to get past her glitz and glamour, her knock-out per-
fumes and her flirtatious games, to what in truth she was – a
gaudy, raddled whore who infects all her partners (vs 1–2, 4–5).

Violent and extreme language to expose a fatal attraction. The
desert saved him (Mark 1:35). The desert place is not escapist but
escape from illusion. It is a real place. Unless we are willing to
turn away for a time from the world, we may never truly find the

world again as God's world. The desert place is any place where the spells can be broken and our eyesight healed. Wherever it is for each of us, it will be a place where distorted vision and compromised minds are cleansed, reordered and brought back in touch again with the mind of Christ (1 Cor 2:10–16). It may be a solitary experience; or we may be better for the company of a few other like-minded, serious-minded Christians, with Bibles, books, pens and paper, for hard thinking and prayer together.

The desert fathers (and mothers) had plenty to say about the essential quality of sincere seriousness. They were shrewd enough to distinguish between what they called 'visitors from Jerusalem' – the genuine seekers, and others they called 'visitors from Babylon' who they thought merely curious and superficial. The latter were given a bowl of soup and sent away. The former were welcome to stay all night in conversation.

Familiarity breeds consent. Our desert place is where we take time to step outside ourselves, to examine ourselves for those signs of overfamiliarity with harmful influences. Where we realise that our 'flirtations with the unthinkable have turned into routines of the unexceptional', and false enchantments have spun their magic over our inner world.

Desert transactions

Let us assume that we agree to the lesson John is demonstrating by his retreat into a desert place; that we agree to practice a desert discipline as an integral part of our own spiritual life; and that we understand why the desert fathers in Egypt 'regarded society as a shipwreck from which each single individual person had to swim for his life. Those were people who believed that to let oneself drift along, passively accepting the tenets and values of what they knew as society, was purely and simply a disaster' (Thomas Merton).[2] What false enchantments might we discover, what aspects of our-end-of-the-twentieth-century 'Babylon' culture might we have assimilated unknowingly, or even willingly? There is at least one area of common concern: our culture is generally hostile towards interior depth, to the felt presence of God, to a vision of the world as luminous with the love and the glory of God.

Secularism, as we are experiencing it, is an 'acid rain of the spirit'. A hundred years ago, the self-styled antichrist Friedrich Nietzsche predicted that once God was removed from a culture, that culture would become steadily hollowed out, or 'weightless'. Karl Marx had earlier noted the same process: 'All that is solid melts into air.' Those were remarkable prophecies whose fulfilment is apparent all around us.

Elizabeth Barrett Browning gave her explanation of God's invitation to Moses, 'Take off your sandals, for the place where you are standing is holy ground' (Exod 3:5). In her paraphrase: 'the earth is ablaze with the fire of God, but only those who see it take their shoes off. The rest sit around and pick blackberries'. We are children of a can-do, make-happen culture which could quickly design and build an ingenious machine to maximise blackberry-picking, but which would see no point at all in sprawling, face down and shoeless, before the Almighty.

Spiritual writer Ronald Rolheiser[3] suggests three attitudes we may well have absorbed from the prevailing culture. He calls them Narcissism, Pragmatism and Unbridled Restlessness.

In Greek legend a beautiful boy, Narcissus, one day saw his own reflection in a pool of water and fell hopelessly in love with himself. Narcissism is an excessive preoccupation with ourselves, which can only make us into self-centred and selfish people. Ours is a time that is obsessed with the self. Self-worship has no doubt always been the essence of sin, but no other age has justified narcissism so enthusiastically; no other culture has been so breathtakingly blunt in rejecting self-denial as a means to spiritual health and embraced the celebration of the self as the highest good. For example, there are currently in print in the US 731 books* whose titles begin with the word 'self': self-image, self-analysis, self-fulfilment, self-help, self-actualisation, self-esteem, etc. It suggests a society that is absorbed in and mesmerised by itself.

Pragmatism values an idea according to its practical usefulness. 'Does it work?' is the all-important test, 'Does it make a difference?' The pragmatist is interested in things that work and are seen to work. Comedian Woody Allen said he was ready to be impressed by God 'if only God would give me some clear sign; like a large deposit in my name at a Swiss bank!' If I spend thirty minutes washing my car, or cutting the grass, at the end I have something to show for it. But if I spend half an hour in prayer and meditation, what actually does it 'do'? What can I point to at the end of the period? The pragmatist is much more concerned with doing than with being. Hence the consensus that activities such as waiting on God in the silence of our minds are an irrelevance, even slightly weird, in the midst of a busy world.

Unbridled Restlessness is spawned out of a secular vision which has no expectations of a transcendent future in the eternity of God's heaven. Therefore we act as if 'all the symphonies must be finished in this life' when, of course, they cannot be. We want to taste all, see all, know all, and if possible, possess all, within the short space between the cradle and the grave. This ambition leaves us busy but bored, full but unfulfilled, a condition the Preacher famously described as 'meaningless' (Eccles 1:1–11). Restlessness is a feature not only of our society but of much church culture also. Greedy for experiences, the people of God repeat Augustine's complaint against himself and his lack of anteriority: 'You, Lord, were within me but I was in the world outside myself.'

Perhaps Rolheiser has touched a nerve. Narcissism, Pragmatism and Unbridled Restlessness are attitudes that could mark the end of us as effective Christians unless we seek the renewing of our minds. And for that transaction to take place, as John and the saints keep telling us, we need to be with God in the desert place.

* (Note for p 117) Source: Mars Hill Resources, 1994, USA.

EXIT BABYLON

Revelation 18

The secret of the *femme fatale*, Rome-Babylon, is at last made clear. She is a dynamic culture of trade and luxury which sucks the nations into an idolatrous materialism (vs 3, 12–13): 'For all the nations have drunk the maddening wines of her adulteries.'

Rome pours out her narcotics of wealth, power and luxury and the people are hooked: 'O great city, dressed in fine linen, purple and scarlet, and glittering with gold, precious stones and pearls!' (v 16).

An addicted world is agog: 'Was there ever a city like this great city?' (v 18).

It is important that we understand what John is *not* saying as he rejoices at the prospect of the downfall of Rome's pervasive materialism. He is not raging against invention, craft, art or science, but against the appalling opaqueness caused by a passionate attachment to things, against materialism. He is not anti-progress or nostalgic for some mythical, golden pre-manufacturing age. He is nowhere calling progress non-spiritual, or equating civilisation with cold rationalism. Someone has observed that there is more love for humanity in electricity and a hygienic water supply than in any amount of spiritual breast-beating; but when greed and fear motivate market forces, the resulting world-view can penetrate our imagination powerfully: 'By your magic spell all the nations were led astray' (v 23).

Bruggemann suggests that 'the imagination of a people is stunted by the influences of an acquisitive, competitive, materialistic society ... such stunting blocks a culture's spiritual potential and creates a religionless public',[1] one which keeps God on the periphery, in a fire-brigade role, and which refuses to take him seriously into its calculations. This is the magic of materialism.

We have no difficulty in making the transition from John's era to our own. On the surface they are so utterly different, but the spirit (the magic) that drives them is the same: 'I am what I have: when I have more, I am a bigger person; when I lose what I had, I am a lot less than I used to be!' Babylonian materialism conjures delusions of autonomy – self-sufficiency, a sort of invincibility – and of inevitable progress: 'I sit as queen ... I will never mourn' (v 7; Isaiah 47:7–8), without any sense of deeper needs (Rev 3:17). Hence the panic, the sense of betrayal, even the desire for revenge against the system that promised so much before the bottom fell out of the world market (17:15–18; 18:9–19). Again, you will recognise the picture at once.

How should a Christian live in Babylon? 'Come out of her, my people' (18:4). But what, in practice, does this mean, when we have no choice but to live in the real world as it is and not as we would wish it to be?

Make ready to go

The cry 'Come out of her' calls upon us to resist the acid of idolatrous materialism by going on the attack and claiming everything for God. If sin is 'matter out of place', it will be overcome by a proper love for things, all things, and close attention to the way we use them, and the value we place on them as God's creation. The way to possess things, says Traherne, is to esteem them, to enjoy the world as 'the beautiful frontispiece of Eternity ... to see thy goodness – contemplate thy glory – rejoice in thy love – be ravished with thy riches – sing thy praises – enjoy thy work – delight in thy highness – possess thy treasures...'[2] With an attitude like this, things, money and power will never become for us God's rivals, nor can they claim our hearts in place of God. We could then be trusted with anything.

From Traherne's beautiful vision we return to the harsh realities of the life we must live in Babylon. Therefore we will seek our answers in Isaiah's messages to God's people exiled in Babylon (Isaiah 40 – 55). Bruggemann calls these messages 'disciplines of readiness' whereby Israel could both live in Babylon and yet make herself ready for freedom. By living this way, God's people could become what Bruggemann calls 'a community of possibility'.[3]

What possibility? God alone knows. The challenge is for us to be free enough from the mind and spirit of Babylon in order to be ready for any possibility in the purposes of God, to 'come out of her' even while we continue to live in her streets.

Disciplines of readiness

1 Beware amnesia!
Recover the memories of our origin in the miracle of Jesus Christ. Babylon will try to tell us that we are no different from other Babylonians. But we are created from the miracle of the resurrection (Isaiah 51:1–2; Rom 4:16–25) by which we see the world as a place where God's power works when we can neither explain nor initiate it.

2 Practice criticism!
To resist assimilation into the prevailing culture we must not grow too cosy with Babylon. Those gods and the magic of materialism make absurd claims; your criticism will insist that these exaggerated promises (Rev 18:12–13) are a hollow joke. Babylon cannot deliver new life, and exiles should be bold enough to say so (Isaiah 46:1–2, 6–7). Only the Lord has the power for life, and he keeps his promises (Isaiah 46:3–4).

3 Live by God's dangerous promises!
The 'queen of Babylon' thinks she is the fertile one: 'I will never be a widow or suffer the loss of children' (Isaiah 47:8). The church in exile is made to feel barren, childless, inferior. But God promises an incredible inversion. But Babylon will be overwhelmed with 'loss of children and widowhood' (Isaiah 47:9), while the church in exile must 'enlarge the place of your tent' because she will teem with children (Isaiah 54:1–8).

4 Sing your new song!
No despair or resigned acceptance of being an insignificant minority people within a great idolatrous system. In Isaiah's new song, the Lord comes like a dangerous fighter, and everything and everyone yields before him. The Lord comes, and everything is altered. Neither death nor life, nor angels or principalities, not

things present nor things to come can overcome the people who share in the Lord's mighty overcoming (Isaiah 42:10–16).

5 Be ready for departure from Babylon!
Act out your defiance of the great empire: 'Depart, depart, go out from there! Touch no unclean thing.' (Isaiah 52:11–12). Make no compromise, accept no pay-offs from the empire. Be what you are – distinctive, other, tapped into a different source of light and power in God. Not a 'coming out' and 'departing' in geographical terms, but in heart and mind, in world-view and in the right use of things, money, time, power. 'Come out', but with dignity, not with haste or panic, because 'the Lord will go before you, the God of Israel will be your rear guard'. You have nothing to fear from the Babylonian police, since you are surrounded by your divine bodyguard: 'You will go out in joy and be led forth in peace' (Isaiah 55:12). Then all creation will sit up and take note when they see the children of God emancipated from oppressive Babylon (Rom 8:19).

Finally, the millstone

Babylon is the picture and type of every godless persecuting power: 'In her was found the blood of prophets and of saints ...' (Rev 18:24). Arrogant and secure in her power and in her teeming business. Suddenly the mighty angel of judgement symbolically hurls a huge millstone into the sea (Rev 18:21; Jer 51:60–63).

> For some of John's readers this passage would have awakened more recent memories of that August night in AD79 when the lamps and gaiety of Pompeii and Herculaneum were extinguished for ever by a pall of volcanic ash. It is not, after all, the heroic sins that bring the downfall of cities, but the sheer heedlessness of approaching disaster.
>
> (Caird)[4]

When? 'Behold, I come like a thief! Blessed is he who stays awake and keeps his clothes with him, so that he may not go naked and be shamefully exposed' (Rev 16:15).

How shall we prepare? By practising 'disciplines of readiness' in order to be God's 'community of possibility'.

EXPLODING THE MYTHS

Revelation 19:1–10

Why is John so obsessed with the idea of Babylon? It has been his dominant motif since chapter 11 of Revelation, and the target of his most vitriolic attacks. He turns language inside out to portray the spirit of Babylon in the most grotesque and offensive imagery.

John loathes Babylon because he fears the possibility of a Babylonian church, one which is compromised, anxious to please the authorities and power hungry while at the same time content with an effete, sentimental faith. A Babylonian church may be concerned for many worthy causes, but it will never show its head above the parapet in defence of the stupendous claims and assertions of Jesus Christ. The spirit of Babylon, however it incarnates itself, poses the greatest threat to the mission of the church in the world.

Consider Babylon as the great biblical metaphor for spiritual oppression and that feeling of exile which believers know in this life. Who in captive Israel could deny that Bel and Nebo had scored a spectacular victory over God? And, similarly, what Christian could deny that there are many people around who seem to enjoy happy lives without any reference to God?

Exiles respond to captivity in different ways. There were famous examples of heroic faithfulness in the Book of Daniel; but others quietly despaired of God, even while maintaining their Jewish religious practices. And certainly there were those who found their Jewishness too distinctive and socially awkward. They simply went with the flow of Babylonian values, and drifted into cultural assimilation. Gradually, inexorably, Babylon colonised their imaginations, until eventually they thought with a Babylonian mind and pictured the world in a Babylonian way.

These three categories of exiles we find among the seven churches (Rev 1 – 3) and in our own situation. Christians today know all about the pressures and inducements to 'conform to the pattern of this world' (Rom 12:2). Babylon is still the *femme fatale* in our spiritual experience (Rev 17). The Babylonian exile is therefore a powerful metaphor for the Christian life: it disconnects the unwary believer from his living spiritual roots in the miracle of Christ's redemptive work. (Beware amnesia!) If that should happen, then, domiciled and domesticated, the exile gratefully accepts bread from the imperial ovens (Isaiah 55:1–3). 'He who feeds me owns me' and very soon the empire has become not a place of exile but home. The assimilation is complete. If this process succeeds (and, as we said earlier, like seduction it is difficult to recognise) we will have become idolatrous people.

> But those who trust in idols
>> who say to images 'You are our gods',
>> will be turned back in utter shame.
>>> (Isaiah 42:17)

What is an idol? That thing or person to whom we yield up the controlling decisions at the centre of our lives; to whom we offer the tiller.

> O let thy sacred will
> All thy delight in me fulfil!
> Let me not think an action mine own way,
> But at thy love shall sway,
> Resigning up the rudder to thy skill.
>> (George Herbert)[1]

If something less than God is enthroned at the centre, then our humanity is skewed; a warp spreads out into the entire world of our being and our relationships. The compass needle goes berserk.

John worries away at the dangerous spiritual influence he terms 'Babylon'. He calls upon all Christians to dare to risk not being Babylonian even though, of necessity, we must live and trade in the great city. And to exert our difference by living in a spirit of worship and celebration of the truth.

> Hallelujah!
> Salvation and glory and power belong to our God,
>> for true and just are his judgements.
>>> (Revelation 19:1–2)

Nothing can withstand the truth revealed in Jesus Christ. What God has done in his Son are his 'judgements', true and just. His truth will engulf all false Babylons (19:3). Augustine, feeling the spiritual heat of his Babylon, pleaded with God, 'Say to my soul, "I am your salvation." Say it so that I may hear it.'

When we hear the Holy Spirit saying it in our hearts, then truth goes on the attack and sings doxology in the streets of the great city (11:1–12).

Subversive worship

Real worship, a participation in 'the roar of a great multitude in heaven' (19:1, 6), subverts the prevailing paganism of our society. Authentic worship in exile is dangerous and radical because it denies imperial power, and it names names and unmasks pretenders:

Not Bel and Nebo, but God.
Not market forces, but God.
Not political power of the Right or the Left, but God.
Not 'me'-centred modernity, but God.
Not pseudo-life and pseudo-power, but the life and power
    of God.

Authentic worship declares that Babylon is judged already. God's mighty angel has thrown his great millstone into the sea, and Babylon is shattered (18:21). God is at work in his world, and the exiles are going home clutching their invitations:

For the wedding of the Lamb has come,
    and his bride has made herself ready...

Blessed are those who are invited to the wedding supper
of the Lamb!

(Revelation 19:7–9)

Thus real worship, as Isaiah and John describe it, is confessional; in it we declare that the living God is the rightful Lord over all creation. As we sing our new songs, those colonising thought-forms absorbed from Babylon are shaken out of our minds, expelled by the greater dynamic of our delight in the almighty love of God in Christ.

This was the doxological testimony of Jesus, 'the faithful and true witness' (3:14) who witnessed to the perfect wisdom of the Father's redeeming way with the world. Now he pours out his Holy Spirit into the prophetic mind of his people (19:10). Prophetic people remain faithful and true witnesses in the midst of idolatry and the distorting activities of the false prophets (16:13–14) and often in the simplest ways.

Young people in a Sheffield church meet for prayer on a Saturday morning, before going off with their brooms to sweep the streets of the parish out of love for God and the people who live there. A Muslim Pakistani taxi driver in Rotherham was recently startled to see a group of people with buckets surround his car. They insisted on washing his windscreen and windows. He tried to pay them, but they refused saying they were Christians from the local church and just wanted to do this for him out of love. The driver told them he had been years in England and this was the first time a Christian had done anything for him. Prophetic witness is different, creative, even slightly unruly!

Confessional worship

When our worship participates in the glory, the hope and the tension of heavenly worship (19:1–9), each Sunday will be an enactment and an anticipation of God's emancipating work for all creation. We have allowed ourselves to believe that our singing is largely an upbeat, feel-good, cheer-up, cathartic and even an escapist activity. But real worship, of the sort we encounter in Revelation, dares to express a new reality, to describe an outrageous and irrepressible truth which dethrones bogus upstart powers and enthrones Jesus Christ as Lord.

> In our exile, we will do well to study our failed singing
> and notice our fatigue and then notice how in our old
> songs, the invitations and possibilities are all there for
> those with freed lips and unadministered tongues.
>
> (Bruggemann)[2]

Worship of this quality becomes the delightful discipline by which exiles make ready to go out with God. We sing the Lord's song in a strange land (Psalm 137:1–4) and we discover that, by our doxological, confessional worship, even this alien land is claimed for God.

> Sing to the Lord a new song,
>> his praise from the ends of the earth,
> you who go down to the sea, and all that is in it,
>> you islands, and all who live in them.
> Let the desert and its towns raise their voices...
> Let them give glory to the Lord
>> and proclaim his praise in the islands.
>
> (Isaiah 42:10–12)

The Lord invades the land of captivity. Goodbye, Babylonian myths.

THE DESTROYERS DESTROYED

Revelation 19:11–21

An adoring mind is tuned to see even more of God. John has stood among the crashing Hallelujahs of the saints who made it all the way through persecution, with Christ, into glory. Alert and attuned, John is able to receive more: 'I saw heaven standing open' (v 11)

Heaven holds no more secrets. We are moving towards the consummation of events, led by the majestic Christ, the warrior Christ, riding out at the head of his people to destroy the destroyers of God's creation. In this kingdom, the king fights from the front. He does not delegate his personal leadership to pastors and bishops, and retire to view events from the far heights of heaven. Christ 'makes war' at the head of his people. His clothes are soaked in blood, his own and theirs. Christ comes with his people to 'pose questions with a hammer', to expose the idols for the hollow things they are. He lays open the illusions of history and the deceits of Babylon through the iconoclastic, prophetic witness of his people in the world.

The vision gathers pace as Christ confronts the beast and its false prophets for judgement:

> With justice he judges and makes war. His eyes are like blazing fire, and on his head are many crowns. He has a name written on him that no-one knows but he himself. He is dressed in a robe dipped in blood, and his name is the Word of God.

> (Revelation 19:11–13)

The names – known and unknowable

The word Jesus spoke, and to which he bore testimony in his life and death, is indistinguishable from the person himself. He *is* the

Word of God (v 13) whose words cut and penetrate like 'a sharp sword' (v 15; Isaiah 49:2; Heb 4:12). Thus the divine rider is pictured establishing God's reign of peace and justice over his enemies by the weapons of the proclamation of the gospel and the 'iron sceptre' of his cross.

But the Word of God will not reveal his unknowable name (Rev 19:12). In the biblical world a name was reckoned to hold the secret essence of a person, his meaning, purpose and sum total. To know a person's name was to gain some control over him. The name performs what it implies: the Saviour saves, the Healer heals, the Guardian guards. There are a mass of magical-medical-miracle name-spells, prayers and incantations on papyri from the New Testament period, in which deities or demons are named with coercive force. One, for example, demands, 'Perform for me all the wishes of my soul. Whatever I say must come to be for I have your name...'

Since Adam moved east of Eden we have been following our instinct for this sort of control over God. We desire, in a very Babylonian way, to make spiritual power serve our ambitions for mastery over creation: 'Nothing meets our needs like need-meeting gods in our own image'. Ever since Adam fell for the oldest lie in the world, to 'be like God' (Gen 3:5), we have tried to manage and manoeuvre the Almighty to our personal advantage. To make the divine names work for us in our love affairs, in the National Lottery, in exams, with an operation coming up. And why not? We need God's help especially at times of crisis. Surely it is not unreasonable to ask him to work for us? To throw ourselves, our needs and longings upon his covenant love is one thing; to use him as an alternative source of power is another. Christ's name is unknowable by us; he is always beyond our exploiting grasp.

Thus our prayer techniques seldom work as promised in the instruction manuals. 'Prayer in' does not equal 'blessings out'. Christ is 'Faithful and True' (Rev 19:11) and will therefore keep all his promises, but notice that he will do 'immeasurably more than all we ask or imagine' (Eph 3:20): Christ, the Word of God, reserves the mystery and the power of his own name.

Blood on the name

We are told the value and weight of Christ's name, and the authority with which it expresses itself in the world:

> On his robe and on his thigh he has this name
>   written:
>   KING OF KINGS AND LORD OF LORDS.
>
> (Revelation 19:16)

And the strange detail that the royal titles are smeared with blood
(v 13) – the blood of Calvary, and the blood of his suffering peo-
ple. This is how Christ rules the world and the processes of history – through the victory of his cross and the faith of his people.
To a watching world, both seem instances of weakness and defeat.
We know them to be 'Christ the power of God and the wisdom of
God' (1 Cor 1:23–25). There is the paradox of the kingdom of
God: visible weakness covers invisible victory in this present age.
We are not permitted to seek other power or different wisdom by
which to make the church appear more credible and 'relevant' to
a sceptical world, for that would be a typically Babylonian policy.
We need to take time with this truth until we are totally convinced
by it, possessed by it: that, by the cross, God is able 'to bring all
things in heaven and on earth together under one head, even
Christ' (Eph 1:10).

The victor still fights

We have traced a succession of judgement events in Revelation in
which God has limited the damage done to creation and cleansed
it from the polluting effects of evil (the seals, trumpets, bowls,
Armageddon). This saving and regenerating principle runs
throughout the present age, and is an expression of God's
covenant commitment to the created order.

But history is hurrying towards its consummation, and God's
judgements will be correspondingly decisive and final. This present vision of the majestic warrior Christ riding out to war against
'the beast and the kings of the earth and their armies' (Rev 19:19),
is declared to be one of the great end-of-time Messianic banquets
(Isaiah 25:6–9) by an 'angel standing in the sun' (v 7), who is

well-placed to observe the significance of events.

After every allowance has been made for the apocalyptic imagery used in this vision of judgement, the basic message is clear: the beast, its false prophet and its company of true believers, who refuse to the very end to turn from their devotion to the beast, are the makers and the purveyors of misery. They loathe the very idea of an eternity in the light of God's presence. For them the loss of his presence is not damnation but a welcome relief. They want to be as far away from him as it is possible to get, as far as hell itself. These are free-choosing, self-choosing people who demand and choose hell and who God must allow to go to hell, in the annihilation which is the absence of his presence.

John is saying these things, and saying them in the most shocking imagery, *so that they need not happen.*

> There are only two kinds of people in the end: those who say to God "Thy will be done", and those to whom God says, in the end "Thy will be done". All that are in hell choose it. Without that self-choice there could be no hell. No soul that seriously and constantly desires joy will ever miss it. Those who seek find. To those who knock it is opened.'
>
> (C S Lewis)[1]

THE MILLENNIAL STANDSTILL

Revelation 20:1–6

After the violence of judgement comes the calm of the millennial standstill. The 'thousand years' are perplexing because now that Satan is comprehensively under lock and key, we learn that God 'must' release him back into circulation again at the end of the millennium to create yet more demonic mayhem (v 3). More than any other passage in Revelation, this one has been fertile ground for all manner of theories and speculations about the sequence of events at the End. We will go with caution in our interpretation!

A problem with time and time bombs

Time in this world is 'fallen' time. We have a sin-damaged history. Our time is the medium in which the Satan-dragon operates. Adam rebelled in this-world time; men and women pursue their selfish interests in it. Our guilt-infected time in irreversible, nor are we able to crawl back through time to extinguish our sinful actions which are deeply embedded in our past, ticking away like time bombs.

> It is time that is empty, haunted by a lost mystery, time
> that aches with restlessness, reaching out beyond itself but
> only to fall back again in futility … As long as the time of
> our life in this world is devoured by the dragon of evil and
> guilt, time has no meaning for us.
>
> (T F Torrance)[1]

Like the rest of the created order, time complains at being implicated in man's rebellious fall: [Time] 'waits in eager expectation for the sons of God to be revealed … that the creation itself will be liberated from its bondage to decay and brought into the glorious freedom of the children of God' (Rom 8:19–21).

Kingdom-of-God-time

The kingdom of God invaded our world in the person of Jesus Christ. He brings the kingdom; he *is* the kingdom. When Christ is in our midst, the kingdom is in our midst; when he is near us, the kingdom is near us (Mark 1:14–15; Luke 17:21). Jesus reigns, 'For he must reign until he has put all his enemies under his feet' (1 Cor 15:25).

Where does he reign? In some timeless, idealised zone? No. Jesus claims this world for himself and his Father. His life, cross and resurrection were this-world events, occurring within this-world time. He overwhelms 'the strong man's [Satan's] house' (Matt 12:29) and sets free his prisoners who now live to the glory of God. Christ burst into our sinful time at a moment described in scripture as 'when the time had fully come' (Gal 4:4). He reigns in the midst of sinful this-world time. John wants to convey this profound truth, that behind the powers and structures of this world there is the victorious kingdom of God and kingdom time. To show that it is a kingdom and a time from which Satan is banished, the dragon is chained and entombed in the Abyss (Rev 20:1–2).

But how can John suggest the reality of the kingdom and God's time which exist behind the facade of this world? He reaches behind our sinful, fallen time to where the past, the present and the future are present in Christ who is the Alpha and the Omega, the beginning and the consummation of time. To represent this reality John sets within his visionary drama a symbolic span of time, perfect, complete, finished, beautifully symmetrical: 'a thousand years'. Millennial time streams out of the throne of God breaking into our present time as if God had struck a tuning fork at the incarnation of his Son. Now its scintillating note goes humming through the cosmos – 'a kind of tune which all things hear, and fear'. Christians hear and fear it. It is experienced as a sharp tension between the old, fallen, this-world time which we inhabit, and the millennial life of Christ's kingdom. Millennial time penetrates this-world time.

On this interpretation, the millennium is a symbol, not a literal span, of a thousand years. We should no more take it as a literal number than we take the ten-headed and seven-horned creature literally. This is an apocalyptic vision that goes behind the scenes to the invisible world, and tries to convey to us how that world impacts on this one. Therefore we are saying that the thousand years is a symbol of Christ's reign during the entire span of time from his incarnation until he comes again. It is a striking image of the message of the entire book.

Christ's reign in the unseen world bears upon this world. What, in practical terms, does this mean for our personal faith?

The thousand years, now

* When Jesus overcame Satan at his incarnation, his victory was total and complete. But it is concealed from the world, a 'veiled manifestation'. God can tear away that veil from one moment to the next, and suddenly we know 'the Lord is here' as Stephen discovered (Acts 7:54–56).

* 'With the Lord a day is like a thousand years, and a thousand years are like a day' (2 Peter 3:8). Our usual arithmetic and notions of fast and slow do not apply to the kingdom: God's thoughts are not our thoughts, nor are his ways our ways. His clocks keep a different time to ours. We should remember when we pray expecting the answer 'Now'. 'Millennium time' implies that we are not to worry and panic at the speed of things.

* Isaiah described 'millennium-life' as an experience of God's regenerating power that strangely reverses the usual down-drag of this-world processes of decay and decline. Exhaustion, ageing, even gravity, are pictured as taken up and overwhelmed by the new life of God:

[The Lord] gives strength to the weary
    and increases the power of the weak.
Even youths grow tired and weary,
    and young men stumble and fall;
but those who hope in the Lord
    will renew their strength.
They will soar on wings like eagles;
    they will run and not grow weary;
    they will walk and not be faint.
                (Isaiah 40:29–31)

- Millennial life is entered by 'the first resurrection' (Rev 20:5–6). By faith the believer is brought into dynamic union and communion with Jesus as Saviour and King. We stand with him in his death and resurrection to new life (Rom 6:1–14). Already, now in this present time, we stand within Christ's resurrection life and authority, symbolised by the thousand years' reign.

> Since, then, you have been raised with Christ, set your hearts on things above, where Christ is seated at the right hand of God ... For you died, and your life is now hidden with Christ in God.
>
> (Colossians 3:1–3)

- The millennium vision reveals the authority and the ministry of all believers in this present life. It is the authority of the 'thousand years reign': participation here and now in the authority of Christ who reigns over the nations – 'they will be priests of God and of Christ and will reign with him for a thousand years' (Rev 20:6). Priestly work involves bringing people to God and bringing God to people, in prayer, worship, witness, service and proclamation of the divine word.

- The millennium vision also tells the truth about the believer's future in eternity. There is a 'first death' – dying with Christ to the emptiness of this world, like, said Jesus, a seed that 'dies' when it is planted. And there is a 'first resurrection' – as the planted seed 'dies' in the ground, it comes to life and flourishes in the fruitfulness of abundant life in Christ (v 5).

  Then comes the categorical assurance: 'The second death has no power over them' (v 6). Physical, biological death is, from the perspective of the thousand years, hardly even an interruption in our journey into the eternity of God's heaven.

Thus the metaphor of the 'thousand year reign' affirms the claim made throughout the book that Christ's Easter laughter rules over all the demonic chaos of the present time.

THE LAST BATTLE

Revelation 20:7–15

We read the next words with incredulous dismay:

> When the thousand years are over, Satan will be released
> from his prison and will go out to deceive the nations in
> the four corners of the earth ...'

(Revelation 20:7–8)

Why would God set Satan free again? Because simply restraining
him behind prison doors is not enough. God will keep his promise
to creation (Romans 8:21) He will cleanse the cosmos of all evil.
But first evil must be drawn out, flushed out into the open. God
will finish this business in a last battle. Under various symbols,
scripture refers to unmastered chaos lying around the edges of
creation and in deep cracks and recesses. God will hunt evil out
for the final conflict.

The mysterious Gog and Magog (Rev 20:8) appear in
Ezekiel's visions where Gog is a northern tribal chief and Magog
is his kingdom. Typically, John does not hesitate to make Magog
into a ferocious personality, along with his partner, Gog. Their
style is to swoop down on unsuspecting victims out of the clear
blue sky. Three times Ezekiel describes Gog suddenly attacking a
totally unprepared Israel (Ezek 38:8–11, 16) at a time when Israel
is enjoying a touch of paradise, an idyllic calm: 'a land of
unwalled villages', 'a peaceful and unsuspecting people – all of
them living without walls and without gates and bars ... my people Israel are living in safety (Ezek 38:11, 14)'. This is a lovely
picture of the freedom from satanic activity during 'the thousand
years'. At the moment of seeming security, Gog strikes.

'Gog and Magog' convey something profound and disturbing
about the world – the sheer tenacity and resilience of evil. Satan
has secret resources in the far corners of his domain 'in the four

corners of the earth … like the sand on the seashore' (Rev 20:8). Even after the succession of judgements, even with Satan himself under lock and key, there remain those pockets of demonic life scattered throughout human society. Satan is able to tap into his 'Gog and Magog' resources in realms beyond our imagining or control.

Alien 3 – tenacious evil

One attempt to symbolise the persistence of evil and its fanatical urge to survive, which is finally overcome only by the sacrificial death of a saviour, is seen in a recent science fiction film. Its imagery is strikingly similar to that of Revelation.

> In Alien 3, the heroine Lieutenant Ripley, played by Sigourney Weaver, takes on for the last time the indefatigable monster-demon-dinosaur-dragon with acid blood. This time she finds herself on a prison planet filled with murderers and human monsters, kept under control only by strict religious practice. So far their religion had been for the purpose of discipline but, when the alien comes, their faith is put to the test.
>
> In this bleak, sombre, brutal and unremitting film, Weaver is plunged into a fight she cannot win. This is signalled by the film's beginning where the man and child she had tried to save in the previous Alien film are brought out dead. Lieutenant Ripley, dissecting the child's body, asks for forgiveness.
>
> At last Ripley discovers what she sensed all along: the seed of death is within her, the alien is in her body, and the alien is a queen which, if it survives will populate worlds with its spawn. All hope gone, Ripley determines to take it to the grave. Pursued by those who want to use her for their own ends, Ripley is offered help and care by one who has the face of a friend. He offers her life, a future. It is a trap and a betrayal. She rejects it, accepting her destiny and throws herself into a burning fiery furnace of molten lead. On the way down the camera follows her fall, arms spread. As the cruciform image descends towards the

flames, the embryo alien bursts forth killing her, She folds over it, a tomb figure, now clutching it to her until she reaches the flames.

What can we say about this? The female (!) saviour takes the source of evil and destroys it in a definitive sacrifice, so that human beings may live. She descends into a hell of flame. The parallels are obvious for us and as Christians we may make as much theological cross-referencing as we please. But the important point is the power of the final scene for the average cinema-goer. Weaver's fall is filmed in slow motion from a number of angles and once she topples from the platform there is no going back, the flames rise up to meet her. She is a large cruciform image who vanishes to a foetal or pupal black blip in a sea of flame. Cost and sacrifice look like this. Salvation looks like this. Tenacious evil looks like this.[1]

Our society is unable to exorcise the demonic residue from within itself. Only God can reach into the depths to deal with it. This is why Gog and Magog are allowed to burst out from nowhere at the end of Christ's millennial reign.

Out of love for his creation God is pictured doing the unthinkable and unleashing Satan. He allows a last desperate spasm of demonic activity, which calls up every last vestige of evil (Rev 20:7–9) for the ultimate battle with heaven; and so to the utter destruction of Satan and his co-conspirators (v 10).

At the great white throne

Then all secrets will be revealed and settled (vs 11–15). All the judgements that mankind has made will be judged at 'the great white throne'. Nothing can stand before God; yet everything must and shall stand there, for scrutiny and for decision, because, to God, everything about us matters, everything has meaning. It really does matter how we live and what we decide about Christ. However difficult this is for modern minds to grasp, we do actually make decisions in this life that affect our eternal destiny.

For us this mind-numbing prospect is alleviated by the fact that our Judge is also our Saviour. He has his judge's books in which he records our works overlooking, nothing. And, as our Saviour, he has his other book: he will forgive anything as he enters our names into the Lamb's 'book of life' (v 12; 13:8; 17:8). Anything, that is, except the rejection of forgiveness. The ultimate, unyielding, impenitence in those who ultimately choose hell. People who, even when they look upon the face of God...

> Lovely face, majestic face, face of beauty, face of flame,
> the face of the Lord God of Israel when he sits upon His
> throne of glory, robed in praise upon His seat of
> splendour.[2]

...still find the presence of God, and the prospect of eternity in his heaven, utterly repellent. Heaven is like a marriage between people who want to be married with all their hearts. Free, mutual consent is fundamental for a real marriage. The moment of death brings us face to face with that final choice, the choice between accepting God and rejecting him.

What else can God do for us? What further inducement can he offer us to make us love his love for us, if this vision of himself is unable to do it? To reject God at this moment would be to reject the source of and the reason for our existence, to choose, of our own free will, the negation of our very being. Those who make this most appalling decision will find themselves, as C S Lewis put it, 'banished from the presence of him who is present everywhere, and erased from the knowledge of him who knows all' (20:14–15).

What is transformed for the new creation (21:1) and what must be abandoned to the flames rests with the Judge of all who is the Redeemer of all.

And yet...

Could we be happy in heaven when some have rejected God?

1 God is a God of infinite love, wisdom and power
There is judgement at the great white throne, but scripture also celebrates the glorious hope that God will 'bring all things in heaven and on earth together under one head, even Christ'. We

cannot synthesise these two doctrines, but we have absolute confidence that the almighty Father will do everything right. We must not set bounds to his infinite generosity or his power.

If 'the whole creation has been groaning as in the pains of child-birth', waiting eagerly for 'the redemption of our bodies' (Rom 8:22–3), is it too much to suggest that part of creation's distress is its awareness that some of its children might choose hell? And if this is so, what does redemption actually mean for creation?

Imagination fails as we ponder these matters. E L Mascall asks us to imagine what he admits is unimaginable in order to illustrate the boundless prodigality of God's love and power:

> I cannot imagine how even God could produce a situation in which I could say, 'I now see that even Belsen doesn't really matter'.
>
> However, let us approach the problem from the other end. Suppose, just suppose, that God's resources are so much beyond all that I can imagine that he can ultimately produce a situation in which I can honestly say, 'I now see that even Belsen doesn't matter, and that this is why he didn't do what I should have done if I had the power, namely, strike the Nazis all dead in order to prevent it.' If this is true – I stress the 'if' – then God's resources must be inexpressibly ampler than anything I am able to conceive.[3]

We must leave the mysteries of eternity, and what goes on between God and each individual person, to his wisdom and love and power.

2 If we are anxious about the existence of hell while there is a heaven...

Can You be Happy when Some Reject God?

> 'What some people say on earth is that the final loss of one soul gives the lie to all the joy of those who are saved.'
> 'Ye see it does not.'
> 'I feel in a way that it ought to.'
> 'That sounds very merciful: but see what lurks behind it.'

'What?'

'The demands of the loveless and the self-imprisoned
that they should be allowed to blackmail the universe: that
till they consent to be happy (on their own terms) no one
else shall taste joy: that theirs should be the final power;
that Hell should be able to veto Heaven.'

'I don't know what I want, Sire.'

'Son, son, it must be one way or the other. Either the day
must come when joy prevails and all the makers of misery
are no longer able to infect it: or else for ever and ever the
makers of misery can destroy in others the happiness they
reject for themselves. I know it has a grand sound to say
ye'll accept no salvation which leaves even one creature in
the dark outside. But watch that sophistry or ye'll make a
Dog in a Manger the tyrant of the universe.'[4]

3 ...we should leave these one-eyed speculations

And get on with the business of preparing to meet our glorious
Lord, to spread the knowledge of his saving gospel and, by the
grace of God, to do all we can to depopulate hell and fill heaven.
This must be our chief business in life, and we can be confident
that in doing so we will be pleasing our Lord.

'I SAW THE UNIVERSE SMILING'

Revelation 21:1–8

God's sustained onslaught on the old corrupt order is finished at last. Christ's millennial reign, which until now has veiled itself behind the flow of history, puts aside all disguise and is revealed in the glories of the new heaven and earth of God's eternal kingdom.

Look at the purity

Look at what and who are *not* allowed into God's new place. All evil and its consequences are symbolically included in a list of seven marks of the old order: the sea (the reservoir of evil, the Abyss), death, grief, crying, pain (vs 1–4), all that lives under God's curse, and night (22:3, 5), and all the dragon's loyal mischief-makers (21:8).

What is left when such things are cancelled? Imagine moving from polluted smog and an acid-rain environment into the intoxicating crystal clarity of alpine air touched only by Swiss meadows in bloom. In fact our metaphor suggests how we may best enter the vision of God's ultimate future – intoxicated.

> 'To the Father, Son and to the Holy Ghost,
> Glory' all paradise began to sing
> So that I was drunk with the sweet song.
>
> What I saw seemed to me to be
> The universe smiling; so my intoxication
> Came both from what I heard and what I saw.
> (Dante)[1]

Laughter alters atmospheres and moods like nothing else. Once hilarity ignites a crowd, it is impossible to stop – as school teachers and preachers well know. Dictators hate comedians. Laughter is our response to a wild, affectionate, or upside-down, but always original way of seeing things. Real humour is genuinely creative and slightly anarchical in its surprising newness. The universe smiling at the new creation – who could have guessed it would be like this!

Look at the relationships

The mention of heaven triggers the question 'Where is it?' If not 'above the bright blue sky' then where? But heaven exists only to the extent that God's presence is there in perfect love. Heaven is the experience of enjoying God forever, a relationship that is the gift of grace from the One who says, 'I am making everything new!' Hence the images of transformed relationships.

Likewise, the 'new Jerusalem' is not a place but a symbol of the people of God living, working, playing, loving together in God's presence. The Holy City has no existence except as the people of God (vs 2, 9–10). An even more ravishing image of people impelled together in love is the wedding, with 'the bride beautifully dressed for her husband' who is Christ (v 2; Eph 5:25–33).

'Now the dwelling of God is with men, and he will live with them. They will be his people and God himself will be with them and be their God' (v 3). Thus all things come together in a kiss. Love is the meaning of the new creation. What can a universe do but smile with delight at what she has become. And we too could allow ourselves the luxury of more delight in God's creation, the theatre of his marvellous drama of redemption. Our joy in creation is therefore a *prophetic* joy since we know that all things are heading towards cosmic transformation:

> Up went the curtain on the world. And what a world! I
> loved it at first sight – and plunged into it head foremost.
> There was no ice to break – the water was warm – and I
> was swimming.
>
> (Violet Bonham-Carter)

Gaelic Christian, Barbara Macphie, describing what she saw from the summit of Ben More, believed that the sun danced on Easter Sunday in joy for a risen Saviour:

The glorious gold-bright sun was after rising on the crests of the great hills, and it was changing colour – green, purple, red, blood-red, white, intense-white, and gold-white, like the glory of the God of the elements to the children of men. It was dancing up and down in exultation at the joyous resurrection of the beloved Saviour of victory.

To be thus privileged, a person must ascend to the top of the highest hill before sunrise, and believe that the God who makes the small blade of grass to grow is the same God who makes the large, massive sun to move.[2]

'Hope is the memory of the future'

Our faith would be nonsense without heaven. There is so much going on with us in this life which demands heaven, like the things we have started but cannot complete. Our existence is full of loose ends. Then there is the craziness. We will find no answers to the damage and grief we encounter this side of the grave. Only heaven will be able to unravel the mess and interpret the mysteriousness of it all. Only the presence of God will satisfy our quest for explanations.

Heaven is not merely a prize for walking faithfully with God; it is where the walk is leading us. It is the meaning of the walk. Heaven is leading us to itself because there the glory of the Lord dwells and we can be satisfied by nothing less. Heaven is 'endless beginning, ceaseless wonder, perpetual resurrection in the inexhausted power of him who everlastingly makes all things new' (Austin Farrer)[3] Hope of heaven is Christ's gift to us. We embrace this hope not to escape this life but, on the contrary, so that hope, flowing back to us, empowers our lives for the present. Hope is the memory of the future.

'...and a new earth'

A new earth will partner a new heaven. However we imagine it, the new creation will mean 'a homely kingdom with earth in it' (Torrance). Planet Earth has a stunning future in God's new order: it is not earmarked to become a sort of creaky, decaying launch pad from which the godly few manage to blast-off into the heavenly realm!

In the Lord's prayer we pray for the earth to become more and more the earth that God intends, mirroring heaven in its delight to do the good pleasure of its Lord, 'on earth as in heaven', uniting the human family to the Godhead. But it will be *the earth*. Adam would recognise it at once. We are saved thereby from falsely spiritualising the future away into a Nirvana-like existence, timeless, changeless, passionless, and certainly monotonous, in which all distinctions and individualities are lost in the ocean of God. These are not biblical notions; they owe more to Buddhism, or to the anxieties of people who at heart distrust this physical creation.

Contrast this with Paul's conviction that 'the creation itself will be liberated from its bondage to decay and brought into the glorious freedom of the children of God' (Rom 8:21). Far from consigning this world to a rubbish tip in some far corner of the universe, the new creation raises its value enormously. It esteems every good thing, every sight and sound, as a system of signs, clues, images, symbols, foretaste, arrangements, which are theophanies, glimpses of God and messages from his other place, heaven. There really is a created correspondence between the two worlds. Hence Jesus could use all nature as images of the invisible world: birds, sheep, seeds, wind, rain, family, bread and wine.

The average child under seven years laughs 400 times a day; the average adult laughs only 14 times. Yet Jesus said we must become like a child if we would see the kingdom of heaven. These are the signs that point to what life is like in the invisible world, and the measure of the spiritual potential of our physical creation.

> Your enjoyment of the world is never right, till every
> morning you awake in Heaven; see yourself in your
> Father's Palace; and look upon the skies, the earth, and the
> air as Celestial Joys: having such a reverend esteem of all,
> as if you were among the Angels. The bride of a monarch,
> in her husband's chamber, hath no such causes of delight
> as you.
> You never enjoy the world aright, until the Sea itself

floweth in your veins, till you are clothed with the heavens, and crowned with the stars: and perceive yourself to be the sole heir of the whole world, and more than so, because men are in it who are every one sole heirs as well as you. Till you can sing and rejoice and delight in God, as misers do in gold, and Kings in sceptres, you never enjoy the world.

(Thomas Traherne)[4]

The new creation – its texture

What will the new order of heaven and earth be made of? This sounds like one of those infant questions that adults are far too insecure to ask; but children ask the really important faith-questions ('Daddy, what does Jesus do all day long?'). The Gospels supply two compelling intimations of the stuff and the texture of the new heaven and earth.

The transfiguration

When Jesus stepped onto the threshold between the visible and invisible worlds, he took our humanity into God with startling effect: 'His face shone like the sun and his clothes became as white as light' (Matt 17:2; 2 Peter 1:16–18). His transfiguration – of his body, his clothes and the world upon which he shines – is the pledge, the promise and first instalment of the eventual transformation of all things.

We carry the foretaste of that future within us already as 'we are being transformed into his likeness with ever-increasing glory, which comes from the Lord, who is the Spirit' (2 Cor 3:18). When, at the end of the time process, the purposes of God in creation and redemption reach consummation, all things will partake of qualities best described by their effect: 'they will shine like the sun', be as 'white as light'. And 'there will be no more night ... for the Lord God will give them light' (Rev 22:5).

The resurrection

Our Lord Jesus rose, in the body, from the dead. The new order triumphs over the old order, the new creation over the old creation. The Jesus who stepped out of the tomb was the same person who died on the cross. In every respect he was encountered by his close followers as the friend, teacher and master they had always known. He spoke, moved, remembered, reasoned, ate with them, like their Lord of the three years' mission. In Luke's account of the resurrection there is that amazing moment when he invites their touch: 'It is I myself! Touch me and see; a ghost does not have flesh and bones, as you see I have' (Luke 24:39).

Christ was the same person, in unbroken continuity with his pre-Calvary self, and yet he was profoundly transformed. He has 'a glorious body', 'a spiritual body'. The man from Galilee is the man 'from heaven' (1 Cor 15:45–58). And 'we shall be like him, for we shall see him as he is' (1 John 3:2).

The future creation relates to the present creation as Christ's present resurrection body relates to his natural body. How? By what sort of energy is such a transformation possible? The answer to these questions does not tell us what and how, but who: 'He who was seated on the throne said, 'I am making everything new!' (Rev 21:5).

At this point high imagination failed:
    But already my desire and my will
    Were being turned like a wheel, all at one speed,
By the love which moves the sun and the other stars
                                        (Dante)[5]

ENDLESS DISCOVERY

Revelation 21:9–27

We would like nothing so much as to be left in peace at this point, to ponder that last vision (vs 1–5), with its sublime immensities of the new creation, the consummation of the entire cosmic drama. Thinking with the imagination is an exhausting business. How much more can our imaginations take? Enough is enough.

But an ecstatic guest at the wedding (v 2) has taken us by the hand, insisting that we should not call it a day just yet, but 'come and look at this cube' (v 9).

The cube

Revelation teems with the rebirth of images. Old Testament images are raised to higher powers and set fresh tasks in this apocalypse. The cube is one instance of this. It first appears in old Israel's tabernacle: the inner sanctuary of God's presence was a cubic space, 30 ft wide, long and high (1 Kings 6:20). The cube's shape symbolises unity, symmetry, harmony, peace, perfection and balance, and the beauty of holiness. In terms of the tabernacle, it was a separate construction, a small consecrated space within a tainted creation. As such the cube spoke of the distance of God's presence and his inaccessible, holy otherness.

Now the cube is taken up and transformed to symbolise the new Jerusalem, the Holy City. It is expanded to a symbolic '12,000 stadia' (about 1,400 miles) in each direction – width, length and height, signifying a limitless cosmic cube (Rev 21:16). While the cube space in the tabernacle represented separation and exclusion, the Holy City of God, by its sheer dimensions, includes all that is capable of being offered to God. The welcome signs are up all over the city gates which are now redundant (v 25).

Divisions, alienation, disharmonies are the curse of our present life. These are healed and reconciled in the peace of God's city. A ruthless vision of that future condition might have eliminated the distinctions between the holy and the secular by simply banishing the secular from the new creation. But in this City of Love even 'the nations' (v 24) who had fought against the Lamb are welcomed, forgiven and granted citizenship of God's city. Conflict gives way to harmony: the sacred and secular, the near and the far, the lion and the lamb, the child and the scorpion, the insider and the outsider, law and grace, heaven and earth, and (most astonishing of all) the Egyptian, the Assyrian and the Israelite will worship together (Isaiah 19:23–25)! God will be the temple for all things – the nations, heaven and earth, the sun and the moon (Rev 21:22–23).

Cube luminosity

The shape and dimensions of the cubic city are a symbol of life with all warping distortions taken out. God dwells in the midst of his people, and the materials used in the construction of the visionary city suggest the qualities of such an existence (vs 11, 18–21). All this fabulous wealth and costly radiance signify not power and prestige of the Babylonian sort, but the glory of the Lord. Whereas in this-world life we struggle to turn back the enveloping fog of neo-materialism, hoping to catch a glimpse of the glory of the Lord, in the new creation his glory is tangible, felt, seen, touched, everywhere, the natural environment. The precious stones and transparent gold are the basic stuff of the Holy City. God is in the midst of our lives: these precious building blocks invite us to come close and touch:

> Take care of the soul: She is turquoise, agate and jasper
> hewn from the throne of glory. May God find her wrapped
> in prayer shawl and frontlets, always dressed like a bride,
> morning after morning.
>
> ('Song at daybreak')[1]

Which is a beautiful way of suggesting that we carry some qualities of our future city within us in the present life. Jesus said,

'Blessed are the peacemakers, for they will be called sons of God' (Matt 5:9). Paul spoke of the church's ministry of reconciliation through the gospel (2 Cor 5:17-21; Col 3:12–15) All this sounds a thoroughly 'cubic' way of living. Our covenanted destiny is life in the city of God; and as life will be then, so we should live now. Christians should be the first to forgive, heal, mend, gather, to go to any lengths to make peace, and to do all in a spirit of boundless generosity and inclusiveness. This is to live the future now; this is to live prophetically.

Cube activity

A popular view of heaven, put about due to a falsely spiritualised and disembodied idea of eternity, is that it will be boring, predictable and very religious, a sort of perpetual vicarage tea party with breaks for prayer meetings. But surely the sheer dynamism of John's vision explodes this nonsense. So, if heaven is not the sensual paradise of Islamic mythology, nor the Nirvana of negated desires, what sort of life awaits us in eternity? Look at the vision and notice who is there:

> The nations will walk by its light, and the kings of the earth will bring their splendour into it … The glory and the honour of the nations will be brought into it.
>
> (Revelation 21:24, 26)

The nations and the kings? They are the heathen we met earlier, trampling the holy city (11:2) and flourishing as trading partners to the great whore of Babylon, growing 'rich from her excessive luxuries' while held under her 'magic spell' (18:3, 23). Christ asserted his authority over them by his own sacrifice and by that of his faithful witnessing people (19:13–15). Now the nations have come under God's redeeming and transforming love. Clearly John did not believe that heaven would be peopled by a small number of martyrs, while the rest of mankind, along with all the accomplishments of civilisation and culture, are dumped into the flames. The nations are streaming in, bringing their goods with them. Only the 'shameful' is debarred from entry (21:27). All else is redeemed, regenerated and transfigured in the light of God's presence. Imagine the creativity, the energy, the music, the invention, the endless discovery. We shall have delightful work to do; our capacities will grow; children will grow. Yet because of the infinity of God, heaven will always be a beginning:

> There is no coming to the end of God; the more we know of him and his ways, the more avenues will open up for further exploration.

> (Austin Farrer)[2]

The cube – a photograph

A young married couple died in a car crash. They were both professional artists, dedicated Christians and, quite simply, striking and wonderful people. Their death, and the manner of it, stunned their hundreds of friends, and not least their church. I preached at their memorial service and, because they were artists who would have loved the abstract symbolism of the cubic city, I took this passage for the sermon. After the service one of the parents, herself an artist and a Christian, told me a remarkable story.

She had seen police photographs of the appalling wreckage of the smashed vehicles in which her son and daughter-in-law died. As she looked at it (and I got the impression that she was not familiar with the cubic symbolism of the heavenly city) she saw in her imagination, rising out of the twisted steel, a cube. She has since painted her vision, and I have a photograph of her picture on my wall. In it the hands of God are drawing a cube of light out of the chaos of the wreckage. And in the centre of the cube, as its secret power, she has painted the open tomb of Christ's resurrection.

> The city does not need the sun or the moon to shine on it, for the glory of God gives it light, and the Lamb is its lamp.

> (Revelation 21:23)

FINALLY, THE BEGINNING

Revelation 22

We have seen paradise regained as the limitless extent of Christ's redemptive work fills the new city of God, with the people of the nations 'ransomed, healed, restored, forgiven', transformed in the almighty love of God who is 'making everything new'. As our Lord Jesus promised, the small mustard seed of the kingdom has grown into a tree that fills the universe, and 'the birds of the air come and perch in its branches' (Matt 13:31–32).

One question remains. Now that paradise is regained, will it be sustained? Could there be a second Fall? John, for the last time, answers with images from the Old Testament.

The first is from Ezekiel, of a river flowing from the throne of God. John recasts it as the river of life 'flowing from the throne of God and the Lamb down the middle of the great street of the city' (Rev 22:1–2). John is no way diminishing the extraordinary power of Ezekiel's original vision, but building on it and taking it further. Ezekiel saw a river flowing southward from the throne of God in the restored temple and eventually reaching the Dead Sea (Ezek 47:1–12). The Dead Sea landscape, where Sodom and Gomorrah were located, is a stark symbol of sterile alienation from the source of all life in God. Ezekiel's river deepened as it travelled on, like the Creator-Saviour's love for an exhausted world. In a boundless out-flowing of life, it renews everything it touches, even overcoming the bleak Dead Sea environment with fresh water from the throne so that the land flourishes and teems with every kind of life:

> Love is in the ascendancy; and unawares, precipitously, a
> waterfall suddenly plunges into the abysmal night.

God pours out his life from the throne, fundamentally involved with all creation, transforming all things, bringing to abundant life what has been sterile and dead. In John's use of this image, he describes the throne as 'of God and the Lamb'. The Creator-Saviour's life flows out to renew the city. Life in the new creation is an experience of continuous renewal; the power of the cross continuously sustains and maintains the people of God in their new life.

The second image is Eden and the tree of life: 'On each side of the river stood the tree of life, bearing twelve crops of fruit ... And the leaves of the tree are for the healing of the nations. No longer will there be any curse' (22:2–3). In Eden the tree of life became to Adam the cause of his fall and the curse of banishment from the garden and God's fellowship. But now the fall is reversed. No curse, no angel barring the way with the flaming sword of judgement, no pain or tears. Not only is the tree of life now accessible, but its leaves are for the healing of the nations. They stream into the new creation still marked by the wounds of their conflict with Christ, the rider on the white horse who smashed them with the 'sharp sword' and 'iron sceptre' of his sovereign love (19:15). The cross is that sceptre, and the cross is the tree of life that heals and turns Christ's enemies into God's friends.

Thus running through the centre of the new city is the ever-lasting potency of the cross of our Lord Jesus Christ, continuously holding the new creation in the love of God. It is very much more than merely a return to the innocence of Eden. 'The Lamb is its lamp' (21:23). Everyone in the new earth and new heaven will know that they have come there only by the cross. The new creation is a redeemed creation.

'I am coming soon'

The ecstatic tour through the visionary drama is complete. Throughout this vast survey of redemption history John has never lost sight of its purpose – to empower Christians to overcome in their daily lives:

> 'Do not seal up the words of the prophecy of this book, because the time is near ... I, Jesus, have sent my angel to give you this testimony for the churches.'
>
> (Revelation 22:10, 16)

We need Revelation in order to live spiritually intelligent and responsible lives in a world gone haywire. It is our Lord's gift to us, to keep us alive to the fact that God has his hand inside the glove of world events. We need it just as urgently to interpret our own personal experiences. Every time a Christian confronts the spirit of Babylon, Revelation is enacted on a personal level. We can know the threat from the Abyss in our own affairs when hell creeps above ground and we encounter those scorpions with human faces. We may even encounter Armageddon whenever we take a stand against the spirit of lying prophecy. In our Lord's esti-mation the quality of our practical lives is the best apologetic for the kingdom (Matt 5:13–16). We can therefore expect the full range of the dragon's repertoire to swing into operation against us.

Promise, invitation, hope

Into this challenging, seemingly exposed and precarious situation of ours, our Lord speaks, 'I am coming soon.' Three times Jesus declares to his people in the world, 'I am coming soon!'

He comes into our conflicts (Rev 22:7)
Tests, trials, conflicts are the norm for the church in a hostile world. Revelation has made this transparently clear. We go into each day not knowing what spiritual challenge it may hold for us. We do know that the Lord has covenanted to meet us in those moments. We have his word on it, 'I am coming soon'.

> Our Lord Jesus did not say -
> You will not be tempested,
> You will not be travailed,
> You will not be afflicted.
> But he said – You will not be overcome.
> (Lady Julian of Norwich)

He comes with his gifts (v 12)
'I am coming soon! My reward is with me.'
　　To his faithful people he brings the reward of entry into the new creation citizenship of the new city of God. Does this refer to

the moment of death? But Jesus is 'the Alpha and the Omega', 'the Beginning and the End'. The End is already present in him; the future has happened already in him (he is the Lord of millennial time, Rev 20). To say that he comes to us now, bringing the reward of entrance into the new heaven, is another way of saying that we possess the future now. Christ is not waiting for the 'End' to arrive: it exists in him already. We reign with him even while fighting for our lives in the streets of Babylon.

He comes into our worship (v 20)

Doxology opened this cosmic drama and tunes everything that follows until all heaven and earth are healed and restored in praise to the Father, Son and Holy Spirit. Here at the end of Revelation we find the church at worship. God will be known to us in worship. The adorable Lord will reveal himself to adoring minds.

For the third time Jesus promises to 'Come', and the assembled congregation, worshipping and expectant, responds, 'Amen, Come, Lord Jesus' ('Maranatha', 1 Cor 16:22).

Come to us, Lord Jesus, as you have promised in the sacrament of the present moment when you appear under cover of ordinary life. Come and transform our ordinariness with your own dear presence, and convince our hearts that we reign with you over all hostile powers.

Come, Lord Jesus, into our worship. Come in the sacrament of this bread and this wine that we break and drink to proclaim the Lord's death until he comes (1 Cor 11:26). Come in your prophetic word, and in our signing and praying. Come, Lord Jesus, in our love for one another.

Revelation is ablaze with boundless hope expressed in that great cry, 'Come!' (Rev 22:17). The Spirit and the bride speak. It is the Spirit-filled church calling to whoever will hear 'Come!'

Who may come?

The thirsty. The only qualification is their desire to drink from the river of life which flows from the throne of God. Christ's victory, the theme of Revelation, is finally expressed as an invitation to all thirsty people – to the world, to the religions of the world, to the pilgrim church, to you and me.

ACKNOWLEDGEMENTS

Doxology first

1 W H Auden, 'Many happy returns', *Collected Shorter Poems*, Faber and Faber Ltd, 1975.

A word to angels

1 Gerard Manley Hopkins, 'Poem 155', *The Poems of Gerard Manley Hopkins*, Oxford University Press, 1978.
2 Hans Wolff, *Anthropology of the Old Testament*, p 76, SCM Press, 1981.
3 C Fitzsimons Allison, *The Cruelty of Heresy*, SPCK, 1994.
4 John Henry Newman, *A Newman Treasury*, p 273, Arlington House, 1975.
5 Auden, 'A healthy spot', *Collected Shorter Poems*.
6 Charles Welsey, 'A charge to keep I have', *Hymns & Psalms*, Methodist Publishing House, 1985.
7 From *Celebrating Common Prayer*, Mowbray, an imprint of Cassell plc, 1992.
8 G K Chesterton, *Defence of Rash Vows,* by permission of Oxford University Press.

Critical height

1 Hopkins, 'Poem 155', *The Poems*.
2 George Herbert, 'King of Glory'.
3 Hardy and Ford, 'Jubilate', *Theology in Praise*, p 76, Darton, Longman & Todd, 1984.

The scroll and the Lamb

1 Michael O'Siadhail, 'Springnight, Dublin 1983', quoted in Hardy and Ford, p 145.

2   Austin Farrer, 'The brink of mystery', *The One Genius*, Anthology, selected by Richard Harris, p 10, SPCK, 1987.

The seals

1   George Macdonald, quoted in *George Macdonald, An Anthology* (No. 311), C S Lewis (ed), Geoffrey Bles.

Who can stand?

1   Hardy & Ford, *Theology*, p 89.
2   C S Lewis, *Voyage to Venus*, ch 16, HarperCollins Publishers.

The arsonists

1   Herbert, 'Prayer (1)', *George Herbert, The Complete English Poems*, Penguin Books Ltd, 1991.

The trumpets

1   Jacques Ellul, *The Ethics of Freedom*, p 299, Mowbray, an imprint of Cassell plc, 1976.
2   G B Caird, *A Commentary on the Revelation*, p 113, A & C Black, 1977.
3   W B Yeats, 'The circus animals desertion', *W B Yeats, Selected Poetry*, Penguin Books Ltd, 1991.

Hybrids from hell

1   Caird, *Commentary*.
2   George Steiner, *In Bluebeard's Castle*, p 63, Faber and Faber Ltd, 1974.
3   Czeslaw Milosz, *Collected Poems*, p 238, Penguin, 1988.

The small scroll

1   Kosuke Koyama, *Three Mile an Hour God*, SCM Press, 1979.

The witnesses

1   Lesslie Newbigin, *The Gospel in a Pluralist Society*, ch 18, SPCK, 1989.

2   Newbigin, *Mission in Christ's Way*, WCC Publications 1987.
3   C E B Cranfield, *Commentary on Mark*, Cambridge University Press, 1963.
4   Gregory Petrov, *The Akathist of Thanksgiving*, English translation by Mother Thekla, reproduced by permission of Chester Music Ltd.

War in heaven

1   Heinrich Schlier, *Principalities and Powers in the New Testament*, Herder-Freiburg, (This small book is a superb study of the subject.)
2   William Empson, 'This last pain', *Collected Poems*, Chatto & Windus, an imprint of Random House UK Ltd, 1984.

Abysmal powers

1   Schlier, *Principalities*, p 76.
2   Thomas Howard, *Hallowed be this House*, p 13. © 1976 Thomas Howard. Reprinted 1989 Ignatius Press, San Francisco. All rights reserved; reprinted with permission of Ignatius Press.

PR for the antichrist

1   James D G Dunn, *Jesus and the Spirit*, p 307, SCM Press, 1975.
2   Schlier, *Principalities*, p 86.
3   Christopher Lasch, quoted in *Genesis* April 1990, Mars Hill Resources, USA.
4   Richard J Neuhaus, quoted in *Genesis* January 1990.

'Where I pay dearly'

1   Farrer, *The One Genius*, Anthology, p 198.
2   John Donne, 'Hymn to my God in my sickness', *John Donne, The Complete English Poems*, Penguin, 1982.
3   Farrer, Anthology, p 122.

Angels of persuasion

1   Solomon Ibn Gabriol (eleventh-century Jewish poet), 'In praise of God', *Hebrew Verse*, p 316, Penguin, 1981.
2   Ephrem (fourth-century poet).
3   Gabriol, 'The Royal Crown'.

View from the far side

1   The Heidelberg Catechism, Karl Barth, *The Heidelberg Catechism for Today*, Epworth Press, 1964.
2   Daivd J Bosch, *Transforming Mission*, Paulist Press 1992.

Armageddon

1   John Milton, Verses 4,5 and 6 of 'The Lord will come and not be slow', *Hymns & Psalms*.

Fatal attractions

1   Auden, *A Certain World*, p 150, Faber and Faber Ltd, 1971.
2   Thomas Merton, *The Wisdom of the Desert*, p 3, New York: New Directions Pub Corp, 1960.
3   Ronald Rolheiser, *The Shattered Lantern*, ch 3, Hodder & Stoughton, 1994.

Exit Babylon

1   Reprinted by permission from *Finally Comes the Poet* by Walter Brueggemann, copyright © 1989 Augsburg Fortress.
2   Thomas Traherne, *The First Century 25–29*, The Faith Press 1960.
3   Brueggemann, 'Disciplines of readiness', *Studies in Isaiah 40–55*, Occasional Paper No. 1, Presbyterian Church (USA), 1988.
4   Caird, *Commentary*.

Exploding the myths

1   Herbert, 'Obedience'.
2   Brueggemann, *Studies*, p 20.

The destroyers destroyed

1   Lewis, *The Great Divorce*, ch 9, HarperCollins Publishers, 1972.

The millennial standstill

1   T F Torrance, *The Apocalypse Today*, p 163, James Clarke 1960.

The last battle

1   From the *Ambassador* January 1996, by permission of the Church of England's Board of Mission & Unity.
2   From The Hekhalot Hymns, The Face of God, *Hebrew Verse*, Penguin Books Ltd.
3   E L Mascall, *The Christian Universe*, p152, Darton, Longman & Todd Ltd, 1967.
4   Lewis, *The Great Divorce*, ch 8.

'I saw the universe smiling'

1   Dante, Paradiso 27, *The Divine Comedy*, C H Sisson (tr), Pan Classics 1981.
2   Barbara Macphie, 'Easter Sunday', *The Sun Dances*, Alexander Carmichael (ed), Floris Books 1960.
3   Farrer, *A Celebration of Faith*, Anthology, p 173. Reproduced by permission of Hodder and Stoughton Ltd.
4   Thomas Traherne, *Centuries I 28, 29*.
5   Dante, Paradiso 33, *The Divine Comedy*, p 499.

Endless discovery

1   'Song at Daybreak', *Hebrew Verse*, p 370.
2   Farrer, *A Celebration*, Anthology, p 173.